THE TO

Other books by Richard Wurmbrand:

The Overcomers (Monarch Publications 1993)
From the Lips of Children (Hodder & Stoughton 1986)
Where Christ Still Suffers (Marshall Pickering 1985)
Little Notes which Like Each Other (Hodder & Stoughton 1976)
Sermons in Solitary Confinement (Marshall Morgan & Scott 1969)
Reaching Towards the Heights (Marshall Morgan & Scott 1985)
Tortured for Christ (Marshall Morgan & Scott 1983)
In God's Underground (Hodder & Stoughton 1969)
In Correspondence with Jesus (Monarch Publications 1990)
Marx: Prophet of Darkness (Marshall Morgan & Scott 1986)
From Torture to Triumph (Monarch Publications 1988)
Alone with God (Hodder & Stoughton 1988)
If Prison Walls Could Speak (Hodder & Stoughton 1972)

Richard Wurmbrand

THE TOTAL
BLESSING

First published in Great Britain 1995
Triangle Books
SPCK
Holy Trinity Church
Marylebone Road
London
NW1 4DU

British Library Cataloguing in Publication Data
A catalogue record for this book is available from the
British Library

ISBN 0-281-04875-4

Photoset by Rowland Phototypesetting Limited,
Bury St Edmunds, Suffolk
Printed in Great Britain by BPC Paperbacks Limited
Member of the British Printing Company Limited

CONTENTS

CONTENTS

Introduction to the Author

A book by Geoffrey Hanks appeared in 1992 in Britain with the title, *70 Great Christians Changing the World* (Christian Focus Publications). Among others it names Peter and Paul, Ignatius, Polycarp, martyrs of old; world-renowned teachers such as Jerome, Augustine, Columbus; Patrick, apostle of the Irish; Francis of Assisi; Wycliffe, Luther, Tyndale; John Knox, Scottish reformer; Ignatius of Loyola; Carey, the father of modern missions; Hudson Taylor, Livingstone, founders of missions in Asia and Africa; Barnardo, founder of orphanages; William Booth of the Salvation Army; Spurgeon and Moody, the great evangelistic preachers.

In this book one chapter is about Richard Wurmbrand. He is counted among the 70 greatest. This tops good, but also very bad reports about him in the world press. Below are a few of these:

No contemporary person has meant so much for the opening of the eyes of the West to what is going on in the Communist camp — except the much decried Wurmbrand. Before Wurmbrand came, we spoke to deaf ears.

> The Revd Michael Bourdeaux, Director of the Institute for
> the Study of Religion and Communism, London

Wurmbrand irritates, but opens our eyes . . . Wurmbrand has got the world to hearken, even if he has sacrificed himself. He has shouted the cry of the martyrs.

> The Revd Ingemar Martinson
> General Secretary of the Slavic Mission, Sweden

Wurmbrand is an Iron Curtain Paul. He is the most authoritative voice of the Underground Church, more than a living martyr.

> *Underground Evangelism*

Since the Sermon on the Mount was delivered, no one has preached with love like Richard Wurmbrand.

> *Haratta*, Finland

I

Wurmbrand has brought to the universal Church a new dimension, reminding it about the martyrs.
Church Times, London

Wurmbrand burst like a fireball across the cool complacency of some.
USA Congressional Record

We were hit by a hurricane called Wurmbrand.
Tablet, New Zealand

We have checked and can say with almost certainty that there has never been a Pastor Wurmbrand in Romania.
Finnish Communist newspaper

The manifestations of Wurmbrand are determined by high emotions, they are without compromise and often naive . . . His judgements about church politics prove a terrifying narrowness . . . The danger of Wurmbrand's grotesque distortions consists in the fact that he calls Christian groups in Eastern Europe to resistance until death . . .
Gerhard Simon in *The Churches in Russia*

In the present Communist regimes strong powers for the humanization of society lie hidden . . . Wurmbrand becomes really dangerous.
Van de Heuwell, then Director of Public Relations, the World Council of Churches

Pastor Richard Wurmbrand possesses a bordello and nine night clubs in the USA.
From the Soviet film, *The Emissaries*, which had as its target the smuggling of religious literature into the USSR, organized by 'Jesus to the Communist World'

Wurmbrand is the devil's mouthpiece.
Arbeiterzeitung, Switzerland

Wurmbrand is a new St John the Baptist . . . a voice crying in the wilderness.
Christianity Today, USA

2

Wurmbrand is a Marxist theologian.   *The Pilgrim*, USA

Wurmbrand is a passionate anti-Communist and anti-Soviet. His books are full of unveiled hatred.
                                                    Several Soviet newspapers

Wurmbrand completely rejects scholarly objectivity.
                                    Reformatorisch Dagbladett, Holland

Wurmbrand is a red pastor.
                                        Vaderland, South Africa

Wurmbrand misuses the pulpit for spreading his political views.
                        The Swedish Bishop Strom in *Dalademokraten*

Wurmbrand is one of the most active voices of anti-Communism.
                        Polititcheskoie Samoabrazovanie, Moscow

Except the Bible, nothing has shaken me like Wurmbrand's *Tortured For Christ*. It is the message of the century. Even more: since the persecution of Christians by Nero, it is the most powerful Act of Martyrs.
                                                    Dr Kurt Koch
                                renowned German evangelical pastor and author

Wurmbrand is broadly charitable in his understanding of God's love and the nature of man. Not even an ounce of contentiousness appears in his books. Perhaps the agony of long imprisonment purges that out of a man.
                                                Alliance Witness, USA

Wurmbrand suffered beastly treatment by the Communists, so he has remained with a confused mind. He is not Evangelical, so he cannot be trusted. He is rather a mystic.
                                            A Dutch Christian magazine

Wurmbrand is intemperate.
                                        Catholic Herald, London

Wurmbrand speaks softly, without flourished comparisons and without dramatic exaggerations ... His concepts of Christianity come from the original sources ... Loud promotion does not correspond to his character. Richard Wurmbrand is surprisingly near to the Nazarene whom he represents. Weak in health, he catches through unyielding spiritual power. He descends from the podium exhausted and has made his audience ashamed rather than inflamed.

Berner Tagblatt, Switzerland

Wurmbrand is a dirty Jew.

Christian Vanguard, USA

Wurmbrand has been pro-Nazi.

Verden Gang, Norway

Wurmbrand, a fascinating and passionate (sometimes even excessively so) personality, appears always firm in the fight against the scepticism of occidental Christianity, which, with rare exceptions, cannot believe that Communism might be a menace for her.

La Suisse, Switzerland

Wurmbrand's book *If that were Christ would you give Him your blanket?* convinces one to give his blanket not only to one's persecuted brother, but even to one's persecutor, so full of love is it.

Nuova Republica, Italy

The denunciations of tortures and barbarisms in the Communist camp made by Wurmbrand are more moving than those of Solzhenitsyn.

Il Citadino, Italy

Wurmbrand's attacks on Communism's treatment of Christian prisoners was viewed by many as sensationalist until Solzhenitsyn's *Gulag Archipelago* confirmed his descriptions of the atrocities.

Daily News, California

Thank God for men like Solzhenitsyn and Wurmbrand. Both have written books on their imprisonment in Communist countries. These books have been made available to us for a reason – a divine warning.

Tacoma News Tribune, USA

Some church leaders in the West attack Pastor Richard Wurmbrand, the leading fighter for the Underground Church, accusing him of lying and exaggerating regarding the atrocities in Communist prisons. I have personally met Christians who sat in prison with Wurmbrand. They told me, 'Not only is everything which Wurmbrand says true, but much, much more. Nobody can describe the ferocious things happening there.'

Mrs Anutza Moise
author of *A ransom for Wurmbrand* in *Morgenbladet*,
Norway

Reverend Richard Wurmbrand still bears the marks on his body of hideous Communist tortures. He is an internationally respected author, lecturer and evangelist.

Boston Herald, USA

The publicity given Solzhenitsyn has brought to light the truth of Wurmbrand's outspoken statements. Should we not back up Wurmbrand and his Christ-like mission to the Communist world?

Reformatio, Switzerland

Both Solzhenitsyn and Wurmbrand are giants in modern church history.

Dagen, Norway

The facts about the author are much simpler: He is an ordinary Christian who lived in very unusual circumstances.

He is a pastor of Jewish descent, who served in Romania in Fascist and Communist times. His wife, Sabina, and he were imprisoned and court-martialled under Fascists. They were also in jail under Communists, the author for fourteen years, his wife for three. Both parents of his wife, three sisters, a brother and six foster children (they count as foster children only because legal adoption was not possible) were killed in the holocaust.

During his term in jail, he never had any books or writing

5

materials. He could only meditate and have spiritual experiences, favoured by the fact that he spent years in solitary confinement.

After the ordeal, Wurmbrand arrived in the West where he founded an international organization dedicated to helping persecuted churches and families of prisoners. It was founded to be the voice of the martyrs: making known their suffering, but also their splendid examples of love and heroism.

The organization has its offices in 40 countries and expands its work to 70.

In different countries it works under different names. In the USA it is called 'The Voice of the Martyrs'. In the UK it has been founded by the Revd Stuart Harris and is named 'Release International'.

Mr Harris was the first Western pastor to come to Romania in a time of fierce persecution; he met secretly with the author to get first-hand information about the suffering church, and brought its message to Great Britain.

The organization provides churches oppressed by Communism and Islam with God's word and literature in 63 languages, legally where possible. Where this is not possible they introduce books by other ways. In some cases they create, at great risk, secret printing presses within countries with oppressive regimes.

Paster Wurmbrand wrote much about the suffering churches and missionary problems. This time he has written a book about God and human life. Most of the thoughts contained in this book come from when he was alone in a cell, 30 feet beneath the earth, never, but never, seeing sun, moon, stars, trees, flowers, birds, butterflies. He never saw any other colour than grey – the grey of the walls and of the prison uniforms. He never heard a voice except the insults of those who watched him.

So don't wonder if some of these thoughts seem strange. They come from a man who lived a strange life.

Tom White
Director of The Voice of the Martyrs, USA

The author welcomes correspondence at: Release International, PO Box 19, Bromley BR2 9TZ.

The Total Blessing

Joseph received a blessing far beyond what his father Jacob imparted to him. We might call it the total blessing: 'The Almighty shall bless thee with blessings of heaven above and blessings of the deep that lie beneath' (Genesis 49.25). This is the blessing in its fullness reserved for the people of God. 'The Lord had blessed Abraham *in all things*' (Genesis 24.1) – not only in material or spiritual matters, but in *all* things.

There is a state of consciousness reserved for the elect of God which will lead only to right actions. This is made possible by becoming a being apart. Samuel said to Saul, 'The spirit of the Lord will come upon thee, and thou shalt be . . . turned into another man' (1 Samuel 10.6). This 'new man' receives a blank cheque from God. 'Do as occasion serve thee, for God is with thee' (v. 7). Saul could do what he liked because 'God gave him another heart' (v. 9).

In the Hebrew Masoretic text, after the word 'man' referring to Saul (v. 22), a large open space is left, because an individual with such privileges from God can hardly be considered simply a man like everyone else. Has he not become something more than human, something approaching a higher, angelic species, in which another ethic and a different sort of relationship with God rule? He is a man blessed in *all* he does. He has not only the blessings of heaven, but also those of the deep.

Through their new birth, a person becomes rooted in the highest Source, which is eternal, and thus raise into heavenly realms everything they touch. With self forgotten, they partake of the divine nature. Passions and evil habits are forsaken, and the way is opened to be blessed *in everything*.

The following story illustrates what is meant by this total blessing. A man played the lottery and won a million. The man who sold him the ticket asked him, 'How did it happen that you chose just the right number?' He replied, 'Well, I am Jewish.' 'What difference did that make?' 'It was decisive,' replied the winner. 'Being Jewish I knew that the number seven must win, because it is the holy number in our books. The seventh day is the Sabbath. There are seven great religious feasts. You find seven all over the Bible. Seven times seven makes 48. So I chose seven hundred and forty eight and became a millionaire.

The salesman in the shop where he had bought the ticket said, 'But Sir, seven times seven makes 49, not 48.'

The winner answered, 'God knows that I am bad at mathematics. He knows what mistakes I would make in multiplication. He willed it that the wrong number I calculated should be just the number I needed to become rich.'

God can give a blessing that makes not only all things work together for good, but all things, even the things that you consider the worst imaginable. In the Old Testament, Joseph was sold by his brothers to be a slave. This resulted in him becoming prime minister and the saviour of his family in which he had been despised.

You can have this blessing, and you can give such blessings to others.

But human beings can impart curses, too. If someone steals some wheat, grinds it, bakes it, and then says a benediction over it, they blaspheme. God said to the priests, 'If ye will not hear, and if ye will not lay it to heart to give glory unto my name, I will even send a curse upon you, and I will curse your blessings' (Malachi 2.2). There are religious services from which it would be wise to flee before the blessing is given.

As for yourself, be cleansed, blessed in *all* you do, blessed with the blessings from above and from the deep. Go to church at least for the blessing. Seek the blessings of righteous people. You will thereby receive a precious reality.

Then share your blessings with others.

God Speaking in Dreams

Brother Lawrence wrote, 'The barque of the Spirit goes forward even in sleep.' We read in Job 33.15–16: 'In a dream, in a vision of the night, when deep sleep falls upon men, in slumberings upon the bed: then (God) opens the ears of men, and seals their instruction.'

Therefore a Christian never sleeps fully. Solomon's bride said, 'I sleep, but my heart wakes.' It is while she sleeps that she hears the voice of her beloved saying, 'Open to me, my sister' (Song of Solomon 5.2). I personally never go to bed without paper and pen near me, which I use to note all my dreams. Occasionally I have dreamt whole sermons and articles, which have often been judged my best. The same was said about Spurgeon.

Why don't more Christians pay attention to their dreams? The practice is very useful, but I must say that in most instances it is not a very pleasant experience.

In Scripture, the second recorded appearance of God in a dream was to Abimelech, king of Gerar (Genesis 20.2). God said to him, 'Behold, thou art but a dead man' – not a message many would be eager to hear. At the same time God informed Abimelech that Abraham, the man who lied to him and endangered his life, was 'a prophet, and he shall pray for thee, and thou shalt live' (v. 7). In his dream-speaking to us, God sometimes contravenes our moral and religious standards.

The first recorded appearance of God in a dream was to Abraham: 'A deep sleep fell upon Abraham; and, lo, an horror of darkness fell upon him' (Genesis 15.12). How many of us would be ready to hear God speaking in dreams if the experience were accompanied by feelings of horror? Furthermore, God gave Abraham unpleasant news: 'Know of a surety that thy seed shall be a stranger in a land that is not theirs, and shall serve them: and they shall afflict them four hundred years'(v. 13).

Would you be willing to accept revelations from God about prolonged suffering for your descendants lasting centuries? Yet such nightmares can be revelations from God.

An angel of the Lord appeared to New Testament Joseph in a dream and told him, 'Arise, and take the young child and his mother, and flee into Egypt, and be thou there until I bring thee word: for Herod will seek the young child to destroy him' (Matthew 2.13). If Joseph had not acted on God's revelations in a dream, the infant Jesus would not have survived. The condition for hearing God's voice in dreams is to be open not only to good news, but to all of God's plans, though some might seem strange and terrible to our human understanding.

We have become accustomed to the notion of having God as a personal Saviour. The expression is not biblical. As a matter of fact, very few people are capable of receiving personal revelations from God. History and biography indicate that God has led his people to victory through dramatic upheavals. And sometimes God's revelations anticipate these dramas. The walk with God involves more than caresses and expressions of love. Anyone who cannot bear the foreknowledge of such dramas should content themselves with the corporate knowledge of the Church.

It is not necessary for everyone to have personal communications. In fact, few can bear them. If we do not have an openness to revelations that may involve great suffering, what we call the guidance of a personal Saviour or of the Holy Spirit may be simple illusion.

Dreams from God can be nightmares, as in the book of Daniel. They can also take the form of erotic imaginings, as in Solomon's Song. Such imagery can be the symbol for capturing something of the inexpressible love relationship existing between the faithful soul and our God.

If the authors of the Bible had not used such thought-forms, the Song of Solomon would never have become part of the canon of Scripture. Today, those same theologians and scholars who consider the Bible infallibly inspired would doubtless reject any prompting to prepare a sermon clothed in erotic language or undergirded with dire predictions for the families of the faithful. Yet drama and nightmares and eroticism can all be the means by which God communicates with us.

Through the prophet Joel God promised that in the last days 'Your old men shall dream dreams, and your young men shall see visions' (Joel 2.28).

What is Truth?

The biblical assertion that Jesus is the truth makes the reason rebel. The classical definition of truth is 'conformity between judgements and reality'. Now, Jesus might be a man or the Son of God or both, but he is in no case an abstraction like 'truth' used in this sense. He is more than the conformity between things and assertions.

To have truth we must go beyond the strict boundaries of reason. As soon as we leave the sphere of the material objects with which we interact daily, we realize how difficult it is to apprehend truth, firstly because the objects of our inquiry do not show themselves to us as they are. It took us thousands of years of intellectual development to discover that both the universe and our bodies are made up of atoms. The atom still hides its mystery from us. So does every person we encounter, not because of any bad intention on their part, but simply because we are all enigmas to ourselves.

Things and persons are 'ex-sistent'. In Latin this word means 'to be outside themselves'. The prodigal son of Jesus' parable who deserted his father, used up his inheritance and ended up herding swine, 'came to himself' (Luke 15.17). Up to this point, he was outside his real self, a toy used and discarded by the world he sought to conquer. Whoever had known him up to that point would not have known the real person, because it was not within himself. It was an object in the hands of others who led him into evil. His real being was divorced from his self. To know him, one would have had to meet him outside of what he appeared to be for a time.

Original sin practically assures that one's first encounter with reality is in the area of 'non-truth'. It is only by virtue of the divine, embodied in Jesus, that we find our rightful place within the sphere of his marvellous creation, rather than as observers of a mirage that presents itself as reality. Jesus enables us to love and appreciate the world as God loved it when he gave his Son for it. This love causes us to apprehend it in truth.

Because individuals can hide their real nature, we may fail to understand them. But like everything in creation, including even hidden objects, they have one common attribute: the very fact of being. They *are*. There are not only good and bad times, there are simply times. And there exists the simple 'there are'. We usually pay attention to accidents and neglect this essential.

Jesus comes from God, whose name is 'I am what I am' (Exodus 3.14). He is the essential Being who exists above transitory accidents. Jesus, his message to mankind, is the truth, above the great non-truth and the small bits of truth on which we live.

When you have Jesus, the truth, you have everything – the whole truth.

Francis of Assisi was once asked, while hoeing his garden, 'What would you do if you knew you would die today?'

He replied, 'I would hoe my garden.'

He had the truth. He was above the world of change and decay; he was within the sphere of reality, where Jesus reigns.

Self-denial

Jesus said, 'If any man will come after me, let him deny himself, and take up his cross' (Luke 9.23). The first thing a Christian has to do is to deny himself. Everything else follows afterwards. If you take up your cross – even if you suffer prison and torture for his name – and have not denied yourself, the sacrifice you bring will only tend to magnify you, make you proud, and destroy your soul.

There is a legend about a dove that, pursued by an eagle, took refuge in Moses' bosom. The eagle demanded the surrender of its prey, arguing that God himself ordained that one creature should live by the sacrifice of another. Moved by its argument but concerned for the dove, Moses gave an equivalent amount of flesh from his own bosom, then freed the dove.

Now, Moses did not tell the story; it is not found in Scripture. Neither are many of his own acts of kindness found in the Pentateuch, which he authored. The self had been denied.

What we perceive as the self is the sum of our performances in life. Some individuals are elated by all the good things they feel they have done; others are depressed by the many sins they have committed; most perceive a mixture of both in their lives.

We have to abolish this image of the self. I am not simply what I perform.

David took Uriah's wife and had Uriah murdered. But he was not what he did. He was 'a man after God's own heart' (Acts 13.22).

Saul of Tarsus persecuted Christians viciously. But he was not what he did. He was one of God's elect, chosen to be an apostle. This election had taken place before the foundation of the world. His life-experiences before his conversion were the developmental steps of an embryonic apostle.

Judas Iscariot went about preaching and healing, after having forsaken all his possessions, as did the other eleven disciples, for Christ's sake. But he too was not what he did. He was the betrayer whose name stands even today for infamy.

A butterfly while in the cocoon looks like a worm. It is not a worm, but a butterfly in process.

The self which has to be denied is the false image we have about our person. There was a Pharisee who really fasted twice a week, gave tithe of all he possessed, and did many other good things. But he was something other than his actions. He was a hypocrite. A publican who extorted from people felt he had good cause not to lift up so much as his eyes to heaven. But God knew him better. He was not what he had done. He was a man justified before God (Luke 18.10–14).

When Jacob and Esau, the children of Rebecca, were not yet born, 'neither having done any good or evil' (Romans 9.11), Jacob was loved and Esau hated by God. They were regarded for what they were, not what they had done.

Do not let your mind be elated by good deeds or driven to despair by irreparable sins. It is wrong to consider the self a résumé of the deeds one has done while playing in the game of life. We become outstanding only when we deny these self-portraits and allow ourselves to be designed and shaped by God.

God does not call himself 'I am what I do'. He does different things, some of which might not be considered lovable. He sends plagues over a country and destroys whole cities. Rather, he says, 'I am what I am' (Exodus 3.14), independently of the outer play of events. Scripture says simply, 'God is love'. Therefore we love him.

Paul, too, says of himself, 'I am what I am' (1 Corinthians 15.10). I am what I am, even if sometimes, driven by forces over which I have no control, I do things contrary to what you might expect.

Once you adopt this attitude, no self remains. Paul could say about himself that it was not he who lived, but Christ lived in him (Galatians 2.20). The Father will reveal the Son of God in you, too, if you grant him access (Galatians 1.16). You will live having him as your self. Then your cross will not crush you, nor will your bearing it make you proud. You will be his disciple indeed.

The Conscious and the Unconscious

Groping for answers, modern psychology has suddenly discovered what Jesus taught two thousand years ago: the necessity of self-denial. The self is our conscious, a small island in the ocean of our unconscious. This little self is not satisfied to be king but acts as if the great unconscious did not even exist. The latter avenges itself for this indignity by emerging in neuroses. Jung formulates Jesus' teaching in other words: 'We must re-centre our personality at a point midway between the conscious and the unconscious' (*Two Essays in Analytic Psychology*).

The conscious self has a dilemma which is at the root of our perplexities, strains, and stresses. It knows it appeared at a certain point in time and will have to disappear sooner or later. Every birth and death is a reminder of this fact.

The unconscious is simply undisturbed by such matters, because it reflects on nothing. It manifests itself in the involuntary fantasy, which contains elements whose existence one had never before suspected. The unconscious is, according to Jung, the invisible player that pushes the conscious personality about like a figure on a chessboard. The unconscious plays, and the conscious worries about things over which it has no control.

A sane self allows the whole entity to speak out as the Bible teaches: 'Love God with *all* your heart, with *all* your soul, with *all* your mind,' not only with the rational, conscious part.

The self is not a unity but a contradictory multiplicity of complexes. A good analogy is the Bible itself, in which are found cold historical facts, genealogies, statistics, geographical data, fiction, poetry, puns, myths, fables, parables, visions, dreams, doubts, utter love and confidence in God, questioning of God's ways, and even blasphemous words written by devout believers. Every part of the soul, even the most hidden, the physically erotic, and the most sublimated love, is manifest in the Bible. God revealed himself to all parts of our psyche, in which there is no distaste for saying unseemly things or reserve for the most holy secrets. Man does not live on bread alone, nor do we live on the rational, the decent, and the moral alone.

Consonant with the very varied needs of the complex self, the Bible offers us all kinds of notions of God: from the God of revenge to the God of love; from the God of the Jews to the Lord of the whole universe; a God who fills meadows with fragrant flowers and who sends plagues, fire, and sulphur from heaven; a God who pities all and who will send the majority of mankind into the bottomless pit. Behind all the images is the God who forbids us to make to ourselves any images of him. He says, 'I am what I am', not what you fancy me to be.

When you have thus forsaken the narrow self, when the whole of you participates in your religion, when you have brought all your sins and vices to be cleansed and all your righteousness and virtues to be attributed to the Creator, then you can die in peace. You die to your opinions, the right ones and the wrong ones, to your preferences, including the preference for religion, to your tastes and will. You die to the world, to its censure or applause. You die also to the judgement of the Church about you. The Church has not only condemned sins but has also burned saints at the stake. You die to the censure and approval of your friends and brethren. Watchman Nee, China's renowned evangelist who died a martyr's death in a Communist prison, was a man excommunicated by the Church.

You desire to be approved only by God. The self has been denied. You have the freedom and joy to be able to bear a cross.

Peter, though taught by Jesus to deny himself, had not done so. Thus, he came to the point where, instead, he denied the Lord he loved.

Everyone has only this choice: to deny yourself or to deny your Master. Be sure you make the right choice!

What Truth is Jesus?

Aristotle in his *Metaphysics* put forth different concepts of truth: *aletheuein*, which means 'nothing forgotten' or 'nothing veiled', and *homoiosin*, which means 'concordance'.

St John's Gospel uses the first person for Jesus' assertion, 'I am the truth'. Our thoughts and words will never be more than thoughts and words. These can only conform to a reality that consists of other elements. Jesus is the representation of this reality in human life, in all its fullness, without forgetting or veiling any part of it. A person who lives in darkness cannot see this reality. But Jesus places us in the light, and at once reality becomes open to our awareness and discernment and available to us for exploration. Gradually we can know it more and more.

Baron Münchausen in the children's story told a lie when he said that he pulled himself out of the mire by his own hair. Likewise, we who are caught in darkness cannot save ourselves from it. Jesus saves us by bringing light, which is the realm of truth.

John lay on the breast of Jesus. Mary Magdalene abandoned herself in expressions of love when she kissed his feet and on at least one occasion sat quietly to listen to him. For the Christian, then, truth is not an intellectual construction, but the abandonment in love to a Person who withholds nothing good from us. Lie quietly in the sun and it will tan you. Lie quietly on Jesus' bosom and truth will envelop and warm you.

All our partial perceptions and fragmented knowledge are non-truth because they do not apprehend the essence of things. With our senses we perceive only the surface of objects. Telescopes and microscopes put us in touch with the surface of normally invisible things, but again only superficially. Partial truth shows us a thing that is. Jesus, the essence of truth, shows us the 'is' of a thing.

The word 'is', one of the most common and unremarkable words of our language, comes from the Sanskrit *asm* – 'to breathe'. Through it the world becomes animated. The word is so sacred that the Hebrews did not use it, as they did not use the name of God. Jesus says, 'I am' (John 19.5,6), and all the soldiers fall to the ground before him. Jesus is the 'is' which is. Therefore he is the truth.

Without Jesus, error is not mere accident, an occasional falling into the mire, but a permanent state. With Jesus you live in the essence of things. Without him you live perforce in the counter-essence. You don't have to tell lies. 'All men are liars' (Psalm 116.11). Without Jesus, you seek to discover true politics, or true science, or true philosophy, without knowing what truth is. How would you recognize it if you met it? It's like seeking a treasure without a map, compass, tools, instructions, or even a description.

When you have Jesus, the Son of the omnipotent God, you do not have to adjust your mind to reality. Reality will conform itself to your mind. Truth for you will become *aletheia* – unveiled.

You are Jesus' beloved. He will lift the veil from your eyes so that you will see truth in all its fullness in his loving eyes and will know it intimately in his tender embrace.

Prayers

When we invoke the sacred name of Jesus, there should be neither the self alone nor Jesus alone, but their union through invocation. All limitations of thought should be transcended.

A person who prays so that prayer becomes the only reality, and the worshipper and the worshipped are no more separate entities, becomes a being who transcends life and death. Every prayer should unite the one who prays and the One to whom he or she prays, so that prayer alone remains. Prayer without this aim is a weak substitute.

Cultures are different. An Oriental Chinese mind is not like a European mind, nor a Gentile like a Jewish mind. For some people, emotions and sentiments make logical reasoning almost impossible, whereas others stoically repudiate emotionalism. But the summit towards which all believers strive is this union in prayer.

Don't allow your sins to be a handicap in your prayers. Jesus did all the good deeds you were intended to do. God sees them as if they were yours. Don't let yourself be troubled if biblical verses seem to indicate, or even an angel of God were to assure you, that you are not among those to whom divine favour is given. Even if you were the most wicked person in the world, call upon the holy name of Jesus and you will be saved. If you call upon him only once after a lifetime full of sin, heaven will be yours.

I know that there are many teachings in the Bible and in the dogmas of the Church that do not make things so easy, but remember that sick people in the early stages can eat almost everything, whereas when they are dying they can hardly sip a few drops of water. The virtues of the first Christians, in the flush of their first love, are no longer the norm for the whole Church. We live in the time of the end when the love of many has waxed cold. God knows the difference and asks only the invocation of the holy name: 'Whoever calls on the name of the Lord shall be saved' (Acts 2.21).

In the hundreds of denominations that exist today, dogmas are many and varied. There is scarcely a layperson who can distinguish the right ones. No one today knows all the commandments and injunctions, nor do we have the power to fulfil them. Call upon the name of the One who said, 'Father, I will that they also, whom Thou hast given Me, be with Me where I am' (John 17.24). Invoke the holy name of Jesus, relying on the fact that the Father will fulfil his wish.

The Christ who vowed never to cast out a sinner who comes to him, however bad they might be, has guaranteed eternal life to all who call upon him. But do so with the earnestness of one crying, 'SOS! Lord, save me!' Yet don't despair if your prayer has not been so earnest. You have called upon his name. The Bible puts no condition that this call must be wholehearted.

While doing your best to ensure that the worshipper, the prayer, and the worshipped become one, believe nevertheless that the simple calling on his name has saving power.

The Simplicity of Moral Problems

Moral problems are really not complicated. The first Christians knew the answers. Pliny, a Roman governor in the second century, reported their standards to the emperor: 'They bind themselves by an oath . . . that they should never commit theft, robbery, or adultery, that they would never break their word, and that they would never deny a trust when called to give it up.'

But it is not enough to do good. The good must also be well done. Thérèse of Lisieux is beloved among Christians not for any great deed but for the fact that she did ordinary things in a grand manner.

To do a good thing well, imitate the sun, that simply shines without waiting to be asked to impart light and warmth. You too should do good as opportunity presents itself, without depending on another to challenge or command you. The good that confronts you is God's thought. It is the reason for your existence. Why do you delay?

What is the good you should do? Whatever flows naturally from the new heart you received at conversion. You cannot find the rule for your attitudes in generalities. It is not located in anything that can be set next to the self and viewed objectively.

Jesus said, 'I am the truth.' The truth, while ultimate, is not a generality. It cannot be anything but an 'I'. It is your 'I' if you are Christlike.

It is well to have confidence in the new creature within, for then your life will consist in doing in the best manner the good works for which you have been predestined by the Father. Therefore, without any delay, be yourself.

A burglar was caught rifling a safe while the alarm was clanging. His captors asked him why he had not fled. He replied that he was hard of hearing.

Life is short. Don't allow yourself to become deaf or blind to the needs around you. While you must be moral, general rules of morality are not always helpful because you are a unique creation intended to fulfil unique purposes. There is a specific role just for you even at this very moment. Listen to the inner voice and follow its leading.

Jeremiah predicted that God would make a new covenant with his people. It specified that his law would be written in their minds and hearts (Jeremiah 31.33).

Tamerlane, savage fourteenth-century conqueror, said, 'Do you think I am only a man? I am the wrath of God.' This is how he viewed himself and this is how he acted. We know we are children of God, whose name is Love. Therefore, act accordingly.

There are ultrasonic generators that are supposed to chase rats from a house through their unpleasant 'sounds'. Likewise the conscience of a child of God rids us of the evil that presses around us.

A problem recognized and defined is a problem half solved. Learn from your mistakes by analysing where you go wrong. Stop for just a few seconds before you act. The pause is part of the music of life, which is a constant flow of good deeds. Six seconds can make an incredible difference. Remember that you are called to be like Christ, who could say, 'I am the truth.'

Be the truth, since you have been created for truth. Lie detectors and truth serum can detect the deep-seated indicators which reveal the fact that one is lying. Such apparatus reveals that adherence to truth and revulsion at lying are deeply rooted in human nature. In modern times we have proved with our technology that truth is part of our creation by God and lying is from the devil, 'the father of lies' (John 8.44).

To be truly moral, withdraw yourself from evil influences. Herod was a king in Christ's day whom God had entrusted with a kingdom. Yet he was ready to give away half of it for a dancer. Instead, he killed a prophet because he allowed his wife to influence the dancer, her daughter, who thus became an accomplice in the murder of John the Baptist. How right was Jesus when he said, 'He who loves father or mother . . . son or daughter more than Me is not worthy of Me' (Matthew 10.37).

To be a hero for Christ, you need not go to a mission field. Your family, factory, school, or office can be your mission field. You can be grand in small things.

We know there exist sins of excess. Therefore the Bible says, 'Be not righteous overmuch' (Ecclesiastes 7.14). There are also sins of omission. Many will go to perdition for neglecting to help the poor and visit prisoners.

The musical sign for atonement, for forgiveness, is the 'natural' sign. A note that has been raised with a 'sharp' sign or lowered with a 'flat' returns to this original pitch by virtue of the natural, which cancels everything else. Likewise, when atonement intervenes, your sins of excess or default are cancelled, as if they had never been committed.

To obtain atonement for your sins from an infinite God and thus receive the promise of eternal life is the supreme sign of morality.

The Sin of Consistency

An individual need not be consistent with what he or she has said, written or done in times past, otherwise no growth would be possible, nor could a person adjust to the demands of changing circumstances. The only consistency required is the proper attitude towards what one considers true, righteous and loving today.

The apostle Paul gives us examples of holy inconsistency. One is the circumcision of his disciple Timothy. Travelling around with an uncircumcised Gentile convert would have hampered the work of evangelization. The Jews who opposed him would have had one more reason to denounce him as a traitor to the religion of his fathers. So foresight and caution were necessary. Paul was dealing with people ready to murder him, as he learned when they wrongly suggested he had taken a Greek into the temple (Acts 21.29; 22.22).

But the same apostle adamantly refused to circumcise Titus (Galatians 2.3) when the danger of theological confusion existed. He was concerned lest others conclude that man is justified before God by rituals of the Jewish law and not by faith alone.

Even the Jewish Christians considered Peter's eating with an uncircumcised man (Acts 11.3) as a serious violation of religious duty. Jesus himself said that he had come only 'to the lost sheep of the house of Israel' (Matthew 15.24), and yet all at once the door was opened wide to the uncircumcised, without asking of them even this token of holy alliance.

The Jewish Christians had become Christians believing that faith in Jesus was the holiest form of Judaism and nothing more. They realized that if circumcision were abolished, the Christian religion would become universal and in time its Jewishness would be absorbed.

Paul was given by God the task to make the Church universal and therefore would not yield to pressure to have Titus circumcised.

In the case of Timothy, Paul accommodated himself prudently to circumstances without endangering the establishment of a universal Church in which Jews and Gentiles were alike. In the case of Titus, a principle was at stake. To concede that Titus must be circumcised would have been an acknowledgement that the sacrifice of Christ alone profits nothing unless the Gentiles fulfilled Jewish ceremonies.

Paul had to assert the principle that in the Christian Church 'there is neither Greek nor Jew, circumcision nor uncircumcision, barbarian, Scythian, bond nor free, but that Christ is all in all' (Colossians 3.11).

If Paul had not been stubborn in certain circumstances, neither slavery nor the caste system would ever have been abolished.

The same desire that made Paul stiff-necked in the case of Titus made him pliable in the case of Timothy. The apostle who wrote: 'I testify to every man that is circumcised . . . Christ is become of no effect to you' (Galatians 5.3,4) nevertheless circumcised a disciple.

Paul was not guilty of the grave sin of consistency with his own beliefs at all times and in all circumstances.

Therefore, be careful of consistency at the expense of adaptability, stubbornness at the expense of flexibility. Be consistent only in your desire for truth at all times, but practising it with the least possible harm to others.

The Commandment to Be One

The structure of the English language makes an exact translation of Genesis 1.9 impossible. A verbatim approximation would be as follows: 'Let gather together [these three English words are one word in Hebrew] the waters under the heaven.' Even before saying what is involved, the commandment is, 'Let them be gathered together'.

Our twentieth-century thinking is quite different. We begin first by listing the things to be united. But the simple act of naming them discourages us from gathering them, and so we abandon our intention altogether.

God's command is, 'Let gather together'. Once all the diverse elements are gathered, it is much simpler to deal with them.

The waters under the heavens were gathered with a certain purpose: to form one sea. (Incidentally, how did Moses, who recorded this information, know that all the waters formed one single sea? We learned this only when Magellan made his discoveries.) Everything was gathered to serve this purpose.

Today there are many stratagems and endeavours to unify Christendom. We fail to succeed because it has not yet been established for what purpose we want to be one.

Jesus long ago designated the overriding reason for unity: 'May they be one that the world may believe' (John 17.21). Too many of us live very comfortably even though the world is made up of unbelievers. Their salvation is not our passion. Therefore our plans for unity fail.

Once a little girl got lost in a huge wheat field, where the wheat was taller than her. Her parents called all the neighbours to help in the search, but in vain, though they shouted and used torches. For two days and nights they hunted. Finally, on the third day the father said to the townspeople, 'Let's all join hands and go through the field in a line.' In no time the child was found. Behind the operation was an anxious father and a common purpose: the child had to be found.

Do we love the world with all our heart? Would we be very unhappy if all but a few were lost? Of what denomination were the people this father gathered to seek his child? It would be foolish even to ask the question. He gathered all who shared his burden and were willing to help. This is what Jesus meant by being one.

An Israeli army unit risked its life to save the Jews hijacked in a plane that was forced down in Entebbe (Uganda). When the rescue plane was on its way home, soldiers and passengers alike sang together in Hebrew Psalm 133: 'Behold, how good and pleasant it is for brethren to dwell together in unity.' What were the religious convictions of the rescuers? Who knows? They belonged to a nation that had experienced the loss of very many innocent victims and were united in their determination to prevent the killing of more Jews. They had a single purpose. Therefore unity was established.

Untold millions – billions – have gone to the grave without salvation because of our divisiveness. This should no longer happen. Think in these terms and your unity with all those who desire to see souls saved will be established.

Several men sitting in a boat observed one of their number boring a hole beneath his seat. 'Why are you doing that?' one of his companions inquired. 'It's none of your business,' he replied. 'I'm boring the hole under *my* seat.'

He was wrong, of course. The water entering through 'his' hole would swamp the whole boat with all its passengers.

Unity would be greatly served if Christians realized what obsolete and often petty questions divided them.

In 1845, 293 Baptists from the Southern states of the USA severed ties with the Northern Baptists in protest over the Yankees' refusal to allow a slaveholder to become a missionary. Slavery has long since been abolished. But today there are 13 million Southern Baptists who continue to be divided from their brethren. As a result of migration, there are now Southern Baptist churches in Alaska near the North Pole, but they are separated from their Northern brethren. Does this make sense?

There is no place for freelancers and 'my-taste' churches in Christendom. Those who love God and mankind need to become one in heart today. The only condition is that unity must be according to God's holy Word, or there can be no peace. God's Word should never be abandoned for unity's sake. But if we are one in Christ, this unity will be revealed in our relationship with others.

== *11* ==

About Being Narrow-minded and Broad-minded

Narrow-mindedness is the object of much scorn. When this takes the form of a joke, it may be acceptable. It is said there was a sign in front of a motel in one of the southern states of America that read, 'Rooms cost $50 a day. For Baptists there is a reduction: they pay only $25.' A traveller, indignant, protested: 'In times past there was racial discrimination; now there is denominational discrimination. Why should Baptists pay only half?' The manager of the motel answered, 'You know, in the South the Baptists are so narrow, they sleep two in one bed.'

When we pass from jokes to reality, narrow-mindedness becomes a virtue. In fact, the Bible endorses it. Paul was so convinced that the gospel he preached was sacrosanct that he wrote: 'Though we, or an angel from heaven, preach any other Gospel to you than that which we have preached unto you, let him be accursed' (Galatians 1.8). He would not have joined ecumenical councils with those who thought differently in theological matters. He would consider them 'accursed'. Today, believers are far removed from this narrow thinking. Most consider broad-mindedness a virtue to be praised.

John the Evangelist knew he had *the* doctrine, besides which there was no other. Therefore he wrote, 'If there come any unto you and bring not *this doctrine* [of Christ], receive him not into your house, neither bid him God speed' (2 John 10). He even adds (v.11), 'He that bids him God speed is partaker of his evil deeds.' He left little room for an ecumenical council. It is told that Cerinthus, a heretic, once entered the house where John was bathing, and the latter left his bath naked and fled, not wishing to be under one roof with a man of another doctrine.

Luther warned, 'The peacock has the garb of an angel and the song of a devil. He is the true picture of a heretic. All heretics can look pious, even angelic.' He was so narrow-minded that he refused to shake hands with Zwingli, with whom he differed about the real presence of Christ in holy communion.

God is all-embracing, but his messengers have always been one-sided. Rarely have they been capable of teamwork. It could scarcely be otherwise, because they have stood alone. Steel columns need no wooden props. God's messengers are pillars in his Church, supporting but unsupported. They can afford to be narrow-minded because they need no one's approval.

Narrow-mindedness does have its negative side, however. Christians are taught to be hospitable. We should be hospitable toward ideas, too, not only toward people, because truth can never be the possession of a single individual. The Church embraces all kinds of individuals, with all sorts of experiences, in many diverse cultures, throughout the centuries. It is obvious they cannot all think alike in every detail.

But we proceed at our peril if we avoid narrow-mindedness when we seek to pass through a strait gate and walk on a narrow way. On the other hand, narrow-mindedness can also hurt the truth.

It is wrong to be narrow-minded and also wrong to be broad-minded. The 'I' that asserts itself should not be. I have to deny myself, denying also the 'I' that denies. As a person embraced by their beloved is no longer conscious of an 'I' and a 'you', so the being embraced by God is neither narrow- nor broad-minded. We lose our 'mindedness' in the holy embrace in which the Eternal and the believer have become one. Here all distinctions between broad-and narrow-mindedness lose their significance, along with the distinction between selfishness and unselfishness.

Why should we not be selfish when our self is God? Why should we not be unselfish when nothing remains of our former self, so that we have nothing to lose?

The one true doctrine, the one true gospel on which Paul and John insisted was this doctrine of oneness with God. Away with the speculations of righteous men about a God outside themselves! These speculations, of narrow-minded bigot or broad-minded liberal, will be false if there is no union with God, in whom problems and divergences disappear.

Therefore don't be narrow-minded, and don't be broad-minded either. Don't be! Blessed is the person whose epitaph is like that of a saint of old: *'Hic jacet nemo'*. (Here lies no one.) Christ is all.

The Little We Know about God

The French say, 'Un dieu défini est un dieu fini.' (A God whom you have defined is a God with whom you have finished.) God cannot be defined or reduced to finite descriptions. To say he is creator is to ignore the fact that he is also sustainer and destroyer. He gives life, but he also kills (1 Samuel 2.6). God is love, but he is also a righteous judge and the God who avenges himself (Revelation 19.2).

It is impossible to describe the fullness of God, because human beings have no frame of reference within which to compare God as he really is with the God we encompass in words. We need to be aware of this difference, even when we say something as simple as 'God is love'. Love is a sentiment common to humans and even some animals. Does any believer consider God a sentiment? To rely on mere words for an understanding of God is like clutching a piece of carbon and calling it a diamond, or scratching a shoe when the foot itches.

Speculations about God can be very hazardous. He is called the Father. His Hebrew name *El* is masculine. But the feminine form *Elah* also occurs in Scripture (1 Samuel 17.9). God compares himself with a woman in Isaiah 49.15: 'Can a woman forget her sucking child, that she should have no compassion on the son of her womb? Yea, they may forget, yet I will not forget thee.'

Jesus said, 'He who has seen me has seen the Father' (John 14.9). Was the Father seen in all the circumstances of Jesus' life? How about his unprovoked outbursts of anger? On one occasion, a Pharisee who had invited Jesus to dinner wondered why he was not washing his hands before eating. But he marvelled without saying anything critical. Jesus, knowing his thoughts, used the occasion to condemn all Pharisees, calling them 'hypocrites'. A lawyer tried to appease him, and he turned on lawyers, accusing them, with the Pharisees, of 'the blood of all the prophets . . . from the blood of Abel to the blood of Zechariah' (Luke 11.37–52). Surely they were innocent; in fact, there were no lawyers and Pharisees when Abel was killed.

Now, such behaviour on the part of Jesus is questionable at best. But a little thought will indicate that it makes sense. He came to this earth to die for humankind. He wanted to be crucified, because the cross was the only way to achieve their salvation from sin. In order to be crucified, he had to be hated. He apparently worked consciously at this. Otherwise why did he heal chronic diseases on the Sabbath when any day of the week would have sufficed? Why cure a man paralysed for thirty-eight years on the one day that would incur the wrath of the priests and Pharisees?

Why were his rebukes so unsparing, so harsh, even if justified? Would not mild rebukes have been more effective? Or did he constantly have in mind a cruel death that presupposed bitter hatred among those who killed him?

To return to the original question, did Jesus represent the Father by hardening the hearts of men against himself? Scripture often records that God hardened the hearts of sinners. Does he actually want to be hated by some? Was his being despised and rejected a continual sacrifice, ultimately beneficial to mankind?

Does God want us to emulate Jesus' attitudes on all occasions? Meister Eckhart wrote, 'God can no more do without us than we can do without him.' Would God's children be more useful to him if they were despised and abhorred rather than successful and admired? There are many questions to ponder.

We have to confess we know little about God, but knowing he exists frees us. We can resign as general managers of the universe.

He has created us and our universe, and even if we don't always feel his presence, we can enjoy what he has given us: air, earth, sky, his creatures. Every ray of sunshine, every wind, every drop of dew, every leaf and flower all speak of him. And so also do love and sorrow, discoveries and failures, agonies and ecstasies, knowledge and the hope to understand later what is obscure for us today.

============ *13* ============

We and Our Enemies

It is almost impossible for consistent Christians not to
have enemies. Because they love the sheep, they shout
against the wolves that would destroy them. Sometimes in their zeal to protect the sheep they prefer
shooting to shouting, destroying to denouncing. This
is how they gain enemies.

We should not avoid having enemies at any cost, but
we should not make them unnecessarily. It is foolish
to make adversaries of those who could be friends.
Some unwisely enter into controversy even with their
partners in faith. Even saints know only in part (1
Corinthians 13.12), which means that each might see a
different part. Therefore divergences arise. It is important not to cultivate a talent for controversy in matters
in which both parties might be right. At such times it
is more useful to mend than to meddle.

There are a few psychological observations that
need to be considered. First, that creative artists do not
readily accept one another. They are lonely peaks. The
same is true of great religious personalities. Luther
would not shake hands with Zwingli, and he despised
Erasmus of Rotterdam. Wesley could not go along with
Whitefield. But not to go along with someone else does
not oblige one to be at loggerheads with them.

Second, that every evidence of superiority engenders
jealousy and often hate. Among those who cannot
understand a work of art, a certain number become
critics for hire. To condemn is much easier than to
comprehend.

The impressionist painters Monet, Renoir, and
Cézanne were called mad, loathsome. The public spat
at their pictures. They did not appreciate the fact that
these new artists painted washerwomen instead of
royalty, haystacks instead of palaces. The artists rarely
sold a painting. Today their canvases fetch millions.

What a catastrophe it would have been if they had spent their time answering their critics! Instead, they painted. There was no weather rough enough to keep Monet from painting outside. He painted on the ice of the Seine, warming his fingers with water from a bottle.

Last century's greatest preacher, Charles Spurgeon, was criticized by the leaders of the Baptist Union of Britain because he was big and they were dwarfs. But he quietly gathered scores of thousands for Christ. We are makers of saints, not wrestlers. A worker for Christ should accept such conflicts without elaborating on them or entering into useless disputes.

On the other hand, if you have to contend with wolves that seek to ravage the flock, then do battle confidently. If you are on God's side, your triumph is sure. You can be wounded by the foe, you cannot be destroyed. Your triumph is sure if you counter the depths of weakness with the wings of faith.

Your triumph is sure if you value the slander against you that resembles truth as your shadow resembles you. At least the contours are real. Slander can serve a good purpose by warning you against the real sins to which you may be exposed.

Your triumph is sure if you don't stoop to using the strategies of your adversaries. Never be hateful like them. Find excuses for them in an attempt to understand the 'why' of their positions. Never exploit their personal sins in order to demean their stand on matters of principle. Remember that you have your own failings before God. If salvation depended on merit, who would escape the pit?

It is said that Conan Doyle sent the following cable to twenty people in public life: 'Everything known; disappear.' All disappeared. Would you have escaped? Then don't uphold sins against others; uphold others, even your adversaries, against their sins.

Armed with such thoughts, you are free to fight for the word of God and for the sheep of his pasture. You will conquer.

14

The Matter of Compromise

Shall we compromise? This is an everyday problem for individual Christians and churches.

Matteo Ricci went to China, mastered classical Chinese, dressed in the garb of a mandarin, and presented Christianity as the fulfilment of Confucianism, whose traditions he allowed to continue. The Jesuits went so far as to use the character *tsi*, the Chinese description of the ceremonies of ancestor-worship, to translate the word 'mass' in their catechism. The formidable power of the non-Christian religions renders any other approach difficult and almost impossible.

William Lucas, Anglican bishop of Masasi (Tanzania) from 1926 to 1944, rejected the old view that the religious systems of 'savages' were the work of the devil and regarded them rather as a preparation for their eventual fulfilment in Christ. The majority of evangelical missionaries, however, have been at the opposite pole. They proclaimed essentially that 'to walk with Christ means to behave like a white man'.

There is something to be said for compromise. Galileo declared on his knees before his inquisitors that he was wrong in claiming the earth moved around the sun. The sun continued to do so in spite of his recantation, and he was able to continue his scientific work for years. Giodanbo Bruno, on the other hand, remained firm and died for his scientific convictions, which he had no time to work out. Who was right?

If you can conquer through compromise, by all means do so. Don't allow the enemy to turn you easily into a martyr.

Joseph could not have been prime minister of Egypt or Daniel of Babylon without some sort of compromise. Both accepted rule of a country in which there existed idolatry and injustice under absolute monarchs. The lions' den into which Daniel was thrown was surely used for others, who may have been innocent victims like himself. He must have had to acquiesce to, or at least overlook, many practices abhorrent to his belief in God and his knowledge of God's requirements for his earthly kingdom.

Much good can get lost in search of unrealizable, ideal solutions. Daniel could not bring about God's kingdom on earth, whereas by standing in high places near the ruling tyrant he could save from death at least a few innocents. More than that, he was able to speak about God to the mighty Nebuchadnezzar, architect of the famous hanging gardens of Babylon (Daniel 4).

Jesus was told about a cruel act of the Roman governor Pontius Pilate, who had killed innocent Galileans who had come to worship in the Temple. To condemn Pilate's crime publicly would not have restored the victims to life and would have put a premature end to the Saviour's ministry. So he chose to respond with a general teaching that all men are sinners and will perish if they don't repent.

No human being or institution can escape the need for occasional compromise, but let us also be aware of its dangers. In 1933, German Christians had a national convention in the presence of Goehring, Hitler's aide. The purpose of the gathering was to purify the Church of Jewish elements and the Old Testament of 'immoral Jewish stories'.

To its shame, the Church compromised with Nazism. In every such situation there arises in the minds of believers the question whether such deviations from the truth have not happened in past centuries as well. A Church that takes a firm, clear-cut stand is surely more reliable.

As individuals and as churches we are faced with having to choose, at turning-points in our lives, the right course to follow. Abraham, while blessed of God, was not always obliged to make the heroic choice, nor on the other hand the devious way of accommodation.

He was free to choose as occasion demanded. Occasionally his choices were wrong, as when he compromised Sarah in Egypt. But his underlying choice was always for God.

'Once to every man and nation comes the moment to decide, in the strife of truth with falsehood, for the good or evil side,' wrote the poet James Russell Lowell. When the alternatives present themselves, the choice has to be made. Let us make it under the guidance of the Holy Spirit and choose the side of good, of God.

15

The Search for Truth

We begin the search for truth without the slightest proof that such an entity has ever existed or still exists. We might imagine that if there was a truth it must have been killed long ago. Jesus asserted, 'I am the truth', and he was crucified.

I once dreamt that some men were quarrelling for a white horse that represented the truth. One man cut it in pieces, which meant it ceased to exist. Then they quarrelled for the pieces of the dead horse. I received the head and was proud until I realized it was the head of a corpse. At that point I awoke.

Nothing is easier than to deceive searchers for truth. At the University of California, an actor was once engaged to deliver a lecture on medicine, a subject about which he knew nothing. The bogus professor was highly appreciated when he spoke eloquently about 'zen-sum' areas and the usefulness of the opera *Tosca* for the study of medicine. Even after the audience was told about the hoax people continued to believe they had learned a lot. We can be seduced by the music of what we hear even if the content is sheer nonsense.

The best and most scholarly sermon may fail to convict if the preacher has an unpleasant voice, is unkempt, or has a stain on his cassock, all of which can distract his hearers' attention.

Who can tell the whole truth? One can never expect exactness from lovers describing the beloved nor an accurate description of truth from one whom it criticizes. You cannot objectively describe someone who hit you in the face when you're seeing stars before your eyes and your ears tingle. The great events of life, whether pleasant or unpleasant, cannot be the object of protocol. The differences in the Gospels simply show how overwhelmed the Evangelists were by their encounter with Jesus.

Often, individuals err because they are not attentive to the difference between truth and fact.

The title of Psalm 52 says it was written by David when a certain Doeg told Saul that David, a fugitive from the king, had been received by the high priest Abimelech, who provided him with food. Doeg had denounced a man who was unrighteously persecuted, and his denunciation led to the killing of many innocents by an enraged Saul. In verse 3, the psalmist says to Doeg, 'Thou lovest lying rather than to speak righteousness.' We would have said that Doeg had told King Saul 'the truth', since he recounted what had actually taken place, but a truth that is harmful to God's elect is a lie, according to the Bible.

The wise man compares truth with 'apples of gold' (Proverb 25.11). Better than seeking the truth is seeking reality about which the truth speaks. A golden apple can be only an ornament. If you are hungry you must sell it in order to have something to eat. We must sell words, even truthful words, in order to have the reality they express.

If we do so, we will recognize that we cannot depend on our good pleasure to know truth. Truth is not the object that we as subject must seek. There exists an eternal truth whose object we ourselves are. We were created by Christ, who is the truth. Before the foundation of the world he chose who would be possessors of truth. He, the truth, has come to seek those lost to the truth. We should not be subjects of the searching, but objects, awaiting the divine seeking.

In the beginning was the Word, not any word, but the one true, reliable Word, and this Word was with God, and this Word was God. This Word became flesh in the person of Jesus Christ, who communicates with us of his own free will. He is love, and love infuses truth in us. It becomes ours by faith and not by intellectual search and investigation.

After that, other advances await us. At primary school children are taught to print letters. But if they continue to write like that as teenagers, they would be considered backward.

In the beginning, you have to establish who is the subject and who the object in the search for truth. You will come to know what an enemy the intellect is, that discriminates subject from object. It is a distinction that the conscious mind makes, but the conscious is only a part of our spiritual being. We have to explore the unconscious as well to achieve completeness. In the unconscious, subject and object are one, and only this oneness can possess the truth.

About Suffering

Don't despair when the stars set. It is a sign that the sun will soon rise. Don't despair when devastating winds blow. Storms pass over the garden of Christ only to spread its perfume. Dante wrote about 'the good suffering that remarries us to God'. When Shakespeare lost love, friendship and health, he wrote *The Tempest*. Humankind would have been poorer without it.

In times of suffering, it is best just to keep quiet. When Jephthah told his daughter that he had promised to sacrifice her to God, her answer was, 'If thou hast opened thy mouth unto the Lord, do to me according to that which has proceeded out of thy mouth' (Judges 11.36). When your heavenly Father decides to sacrifice you, your joy, your health, your liberty, your position, for some mysterious purpose of his, be like Jephthah's daughter even if you do not understand his purposes. Remember that from the burning ovens of Auschwitz, where Jews suffered, and from Communist and Muslim jails, in which Christians still suffer for their faith, beacons of warning and hope shine.

Remain quiet during the time of deepest suffering, when a loved one dies. Jesus said to his disciples on the occasion of the Last Supper, 'It is expedient for you that I go away' (John 16.7). These words might be said about everyone who dies.

God loves you. Why would he allow you to lose someone precious if it were not for your good and theirs? Those who live in the invisible world of the spirit view the death of a friend as a release, not as a separation. Those who die pass from shadows and images to truth. Even those in hell finally know the truth.

When John Chrysostom arrived after a three-month journey at Comana, the place to which he had been deported, Basilicus, who had been martyred there, appeared to him in vision saying, 'Courage, brother, tomorrow we will be together.' He died the next day saying as his last words, 'Glory to God, Amen.' In psychological depths inaccessible to our consciousness, the dead whom we mourn might have had a similar vision.

Face everything quietly. When the stars set, the sun rises.

17

The Angels of Suffering

'The Lord sent fiery serpents among the people' (Numbers 21.6). What does this Bible verse mean? Fiery serpents as such do not exist. In fact, the Hebrew original has no such expression. Instead, we read, *'Nahashim seraphim'*. *Nahashim* means 'serpents', and *seraphim* is the word for a special class of angels. So the serpents that bit the Jews were in reality embodiments of angels of God. John in Revelation describes four beasts, one like a lion, the second like a calf, the third like an eagle, and the fourth like a man (Revelation 4.6–8). So angels can have the forms of animals. Why not the shape of a serpent? The psalmist says, 'The angel of the Lord encamps round about them that fear him' (Psalm 34.7). Only if he has the shape of a serpent can he do this.

The serpents that hurt the Jews were either angels of God or beings directed by them. From this we learn to see our friends the angels behind even serious troubles.

God writes straight on crooked lines. The most adverse happenings in the lives of his children work together for good. Not every Christian is ready to break his bottle of perfume to anoint Jesus, as did Mary Magdalene. If angels did not break our bottles by giving us suffering, the fragrance would not be released.

Therefore, don't murmur and complain when a cross is given to you. Atrocious suffering defies explanation. Rather, ask what is the purpose of the cross. Is it not to make us angel-like? A cross can be a splendid opportunity. When Jesus was crucified, he hung between two thieves. One asked to be taken down from the cross, the other to be taken up. Suffering provides us with the same choice.

Those who wish to be taken up do not denounce those who have done mischief to them; they don't even wonder about the hardships of life. They know we are a sentenced race. God said to Adam, 'In sorrow you shall eat of the ground all the days of your life' (Genesis 3.17). We should be thankful for the few days without hardship.

The person who 'goes up' when suffering asks, 'Do I deserve better? Have I fulfilled the commandments that are connected to blessings?' They say what the repentant thief said to the unrepentant who cursed: 'Do you not fear God, seeing you are in the same condemnation? And we indeed justly, for we receive the due reward of our deeds, but this man [Jesus] has done nothing amiss' (Luke 23.41).

The Christian is free from the curse of sin through the atoning sacrifice of Christ. The evils we encounter are unfinished good. Whenever we weep a tear, a gem is added to our crown.

The suffering saints are the jewels of the Church. In a dream I once saw myself in a chapel. All those at the altar and in the front rows wore plain clothes. Only the sick and the poor in the rear wore priestly ornaments. The suffering saints are the teachers, those at ease the learners.

Don't be afraid to suffer.

18

Sharing His Divinity

Jesus should not be an unknown person remote from us. To bring him nearer, we should love everyone, whatever their defects, as if they were Jesus; listen to every word, even if it is sinful and blasphemous, as if it were a prayer, in consideration of the suffering and ignorance from which it springs; and behave in every place as if it were heaven.

Remember first of all that Jesus lived the life of a man from an oppressed class in an oppressed nation, that he therefore has close ties with all the oppressed and sees in those who hunger, thirst, are naked, imprisoned, and injured his little brothers and sisters. This will familiarize you with Jesus.

The Holy Spirit is compared in Scripture to rivers of living water. We can swim *in* them as in the ocean, because these rivers are accessible to everyone. But if we have the wrong attitude, we can swim *through* them like submarines in the sea, sealed off from their healing influence and encased in our own atmosphere.

The Roman philosopher of antiquity Cato said long ago, 'The soul of a lover lives in another's body.' Jesus is the supreme lover. You don't have to seek him far. He lives within you, as you live in him, if you are his.

This oneness with him gives a person the sense of utter freedom from another's judgements. What do the opinions of others count if Jesus' contemporaries called him a devil, a madman, a being with an unclean spirit?

Belief in him also unites you in fellowship with other believers throughout the whole world, even if they differ from you. They might not witness openly for the faith as you do, but this does not make them inferior. Jesus had his hidden disciples who, while hiding their faith, were still considered his. Nicodemus and Joseph of Arimathea were among them. The apostle John could not have trumpeted his faith in Jerusalem or he would never have been in such good standing with the high priest Caiaphas that he was allowed to enter the heavily guarded temple with his friend Peter during Jesus' trial. Such a privilege was granted only to those considered reliable by the high priest. Under the circumstances, a known disciple of Jesus would not have been admitted.

You will have the friendship not only of those who say they are Christians, but also of those who do not make this public confession. You will have the fellowship of people of other persuasions who also love Jesus. A blind man healed by the Saviour was asked, 'What do you say of him that has opened your eyes?' His only answer was, 'He is a prophet' (John 9.17). Reformed Jews, Unitarians, and Muslims could subscribe to this statement. The healed blind man did not believe in Jesus according to the Athanasian creed, but neither did anyone else in the first centuries of the Christian Church. Yet they were disciples and were received by God as such. Those who may not understand the development of Christology in the Church will be your friends, too.

The blind man's intuition about who Jesus was might have been deficient, but he had the right spirit. He expressed only thankfulness to God for having been healed, without reproaching his Creator for his previous blindness.

What reproaches can a lover bring against the beloved? Desdemona did not rebuke Othello even for killing her, but continued to love him. This is the logic of romance, and no romance could ever equal that between the believing soul and the Man of Calvary.

All are called to become his brides. He excludes no one but those who exclude themselves. Our sinfulness is no hindrance, since our guilt has been transferred to the Son of God. To make us clean, He declared himself guilty for what we have done. There is no barrier between us.

An identification between Christ and the individual takes place. God said to Abraham, 'In thee shall all families of the earth be blessed' (Genesis 12.3). The Messiah, Abraham's descendant, is here intended, but the Bible makes no distinction between him and his ancestor. When you are blessed in Jesus, you are blessed in Abraham and vice versa. The first Christians had a proverb: 'Whoever sees a brother sees God.'

Jesus is ever willing to share his divinity with humanity. In fact, he often speaks about himself in the third person. When we do so, we are using his own language, though it is best to think about him as our 'I'.

In loving him, we love the best that is in us. Incredibly, the weaker our love and the greater the danger that we might lose it altogether, the more saving grace is granted, until we become one with him, as he and the Father are one.

Attitude towards Law

There are two kinds of law: those made by people, and those for which people are made. The latter come from God and must take precedence.

Such commandments are, however, individualized. The Lord said to John, 'Write the things which thou hast seen' (Revelation 1.19). Paul, on the other hand, heard in heaven 'unspeakable words, which it is not lawful for a man to utter' (2 Corinthians 12.4). We can only hint at the main characteristics of such forbidden words: they always have a dual character.

One and the same biblical word expressed the plus and the minus, the positive and the negative. For instance, the Greek word *afes*, used in the Lord's Prayer for 'forgive us our trespasses', means also 'to leave'. Thus we have two sides within us: one desires to keep sins because they are sweet; another wants to get rid of them. When you recite the 'Our Father' in the original Greek, both sides of your personality have had their say: 'Leave us our trespasses' and 'Forgive us . . .' Such words are difficult for the nonspiritual to comprehend.

God's laws have a dual character. On one side is the law of love. Since we live in a doomed world, mutual understanding is in the supreme interest of the whole of mankind. We must unite and love each other even where union seems illogical. Two enemies on a sinking ship should at least unite their efforts so that they can survive to continue their quarrel.

Whoever stands for love between races, nations, religions, parties, classes, generations or individuals, and suffers for this cause resembles Christ, regardless of their convictions in matters of faith.

Love is in our best interest even if it brings suffering, first of all because love is more beautiful than hatred. It is good to give to the poor, not only for the sake of the

53

poor but because wealth destroys character and often denies one entrance into heaven.

If several individuals plot to slander you, go along with them. No one believes the self-accusations of a person who claims to be evil. Jesus said, 'Agree with your adversary quickly, while you are on the way with him' (Matthew 5.25).

Love your enemies too. If you cannot forgive them for Christ's sake, then do so for the sake of your gallbladder and stomach. Kindness is never wasted. At the very least it profits the giver. Anyone who does not forgive burns the bridge over which they will have to pass. None of us can enter heaven except as forgiven sinners.

Know yourself and acknowledge that if it is difficult for you to forgive an enemy's mistake, the reason could be that your enemy has witnessed your own.

Love is the law for which we were made.

This is one aspect of what you hear in heaven. There exists another side to the matter.

Only fools are honest with the dishonest. A policeman who made it a principle to deal honestly with terrorists, spies, and drug-smugglers would never catch a criminal. There cannot exist one general rule of behaviour towards all men. With some we have to use cunning.

The Lord teaches us to be as wise as serpents (Matthew 10.16). The New Testament employs here the same word used in the Septuagint for the devil in Genesis 3.1. He meant that we should at least equal the devils in wisdom, though of another quality.

Wisdom will sometimes make us add to the common law. God told Adam not to eat of the tree of the knowledge of good and evil (Genesis 2.17). Apparently Adam then instructed weaker Eve, 'You shall not eat of it, neither shall you touch it' (Genesis 3.1). This is how we have to instruct those who are young in the faith. We raise a fence around the commandments and add other restrictions.

Wisdom occasionally obliges us to enlarge the possibilities of action. One need not feel guilty for telling an untruth in favour of the persecuted. Undue sympathy for criminals can become a crime in itself by encouraging their behaviour. There can be no peace in a state without putting down rebellion.

'The Lord raised unto the children of Israel a deliverer, Ehud' (Judges 3.15). This man, a left-handed Benjaminite, used deceit to kill their oppressor. To judge his deed, we have to remember that he was raised up as a deliverer by God. Origen says the very name of Ehud means 'glory', and Ehud is the male form of Jehudah, the name of God's land.

Ehud killed the tyrant Eglon with his left hand. He had hidden his dagger upon his right thigh, where it would have passed unobserved. In the biblical Greek the word for 'left' is *aristeros*, which means 'the noblest' side. The infirmity of Ehud became an instrument of God. To obtain a private audience with the king, he said, 'I have a message from God unto thee' (Judges 33.20). Eglon arose from his seat to show respect when he heard the name 'God', and in that moment he was killed.

Origen, one of the famous teachers of the Church, praises the prevarications of Ehud. St Basil the Great also considers Ehud's lie justified. The law of God has a dual character. A state of war frees one from the obligation of truthfulness. This rule stands as well for the war in which the Church is engaged in countries with religious persecution.

Mahatma Gandhi said he would not tell a lie even if by so doing they could save the souls of the whole world. This is wrong. Love is better than truth. The law of love is two-sided.

Not Acting

The predominant question in the minds of many believers is simply: What is the right course of action to follow? The right course may very well be not to act.

Jesus might have asked the Father this question when he received the reply, 'Sit thou at my right hand, until I make thine enemies thy footstool' (Psalm 110.1). This did not mean sitting quietly for a short period but for thousands of years while the enemies continued to poison humankind with lying doctrines, destroy millions of believers, and bring unspeakable suffering upon the whole creation.

What should one do when confronted with a drama of such proportions? Before expecting an answer to such a question, ask yourself if it is legitimate, if it is proper, to do anything. God is not always impressed with our doings. His advice is 'Sit'.

This is a teaching, not a law. The Hebrew word *Torah*, the name for the five books of Moses, means 'teaching'. It has been falsely translated as 'law' in the Greek version of the Old Testament known as the Septuagint. Generally, the Bible does not impose commandments; rather, it gives counsel about the best way to follow God's desires. It even provides several options.

Patience must not mean passiveness. If the psalmist says 'Sit', it does not mean you should do nothing. Many good works can be done with a relaxed spirit and relaxed muscles, just as one sits.

Do what you need to do, but do so remaining comfortable, at ease, not worrying if others will approve your actions. To reach an objective you might have to apply methods some people will not appreciate. The main test is whether you bring home your trophy.

Before asking yourself what you should do, decide whether you can do it with peace of mind. God kept the Sabbath. A person who believes that he can do anything useful without keeping the Sabbath fools himself. When God created the world and organized it, he knew that Adam and Eve were in great danger, because the serpent was in Eden. Notwithstanding, he rested. You can do the same.

You may say you are in great shape and need no rest. But what if the Sabbath needs you? The Talmud says that the days of the week once put their case to God. Sunday had Monday as a friend, Tuesday had Wednesday, Thursday was on good terms with Friday. Only Saturday was alone. So God gave his holy people to be the Sabbath's friend. You might not need rest, but rest needs you. Rest not for your own sake, but in order that rest, repose, and quietness might not feel rejected and abandoned. The Sabbath will reward your love and will make the smallest deeds fruitful.

Because we do not rest properly, we improvise. Abraham was in a hurry to fulfil God's promise and so procreated a son by Hagar instead of waiting for God's timing – and the world even today is paying the price. But God keeps his promises and can provide an heir in old age. Right actions can wait. We can take our time.

It is better not to attempt too many different enterprises, but rather to do one good thing over and over until we can do it really well. John Wesley as a boy was not good at mathematics. Once he asked his mother the same question twenty times. His father got angry at her: 'Stop repeating the same thing. You have already given him the answer nineteen times.' His mother replied, 'Isn't it better to say it twenty times, instead of allowing the nineteen efforts to be lost?'

Don't look into any textbook or code to inspire you to right actions. Saul was the king, so Doeg was loyal to him. He told the king the truth about David and his companions and added that they had been fed at the house of Abimelech, the high priest. But the inspired writer calls him a liar and a lover of evil. In God's eyes it is a lie to make a truthful denunciation to the legitimate king if he is a tyrant rejected by God.

God promises you a new heart. If you don't feel entitled to one, then take it from him by force. The Lord says, 'The kingdom of heaven suffers violence, and the violent take it by force' (Matthew 11.12). Once the kingdom of heaven is within, you will need no textbooks to guide you. Know that even in the Bible some commandments are given in irony, such as 'Fill up the measure of your fathers' (Matthew 23.32). Go after your new character, not after verses.

A word of caution is in order. Be aware of the fact that as often as you do something amiss, Jesus is asked, 'Why do thy disciples transgress?' (Matthew 15.2). This question is posed even now in heaven. Don't put him in an embarrassing situation.

Don't spend a lot of time trying to decide what to do. Jesus says, 'Take the fish that first comes up' (Matthew 17.27). You might find it difficult just to sit still. But if you can, it will be your first opportunity to do quietly something that is the right action for you.

Right Actions

If you have good intentions, it is advisable not to try and implement them immediately with good deeds. These may be premature.

A tin soldier once wanted to change the world so that everyone would be happy, but he forgot he was made of cheap metal. As soon as he entered the fire of battle, he melted. Changing yourself is more difficult than changing the world. To do so you must be made of very resistant material.

First, you must be a new person who has repented of your sins. The author of the rabbinical book *Levitic Rabba* writes,

> Whence is it derived that if one repents it is imputed to him as if he had gone up to Jerusalem, built the Temple, erected an altar, and offered upon it all the sacrifices enumerated in the Law? From the text, 'The sacrifices of God are a broken spirit' (Psalm 51.17).

Then, begin by offering to God the sacrifice of a broken spirit.

The German philosopher Karl Jaspers said, 'Crucial for man is his attitude toward failure, because the way in which man approaches his failure determines what he will become.'

Before starting to perform any good deed, acknowledge that past actions have been wrong. Repent of them and believe that Jesus' sacrifice has erased them and all their evil consequences. Then you are ready to proceed. But always remember that even the new creature is only human, limited not only by the flow of external circumstances, but also by an inner stream with a predetermined bed, the only channel in which it can flow.

The French have an expression *'violon d'Ingres'*.

Ingres was a gifted painter, whose few creations are in the Louvre. They are few because he believed himself to be a violinist. The tragedy is that when he played the instrument, all the neighbours had to plug their ears, so unbearable was his musicianship. Ingres was a man who did not know his talent.

It is important that you know what is possible for you and what is not.

Eisenhower told Khrushchev, 'In our country we are all equal. Anyone can become president.' The dictator pointed to a man who was just sweeping the garden in front of the White House and asked, 'Can you really assert that such a person can become president?' Eisenhower replied, 'Not this man; he sweeps against the wind.'

Every human being has certain possibilities, certain doors to which he has the key. Other doors are completely closed to him. Jesus says again and again, 'Go *your* way!' Your way is the only one in which you can be successful.

Don't try to change your behaviour. Actions are the shadow cast by a personality. Spend all such endeavours in changing your personality.

Work at this quietly. There is no hurry. There is no great distance to traverse. Even if you have committed atrocious crimes you are not far from God. Jesus tells us about a son who forsook his father 'and took his journey into a far country' (Luke 15.13). Such a journey is possible on earth, but which country or state of soul is far from the heavenly Father?

We are called to enter a place we never left. The return is easy. When the prodigal son 'came to himself' (v. 17), very soon he also found himself in his father's arms. What you really need to know is that 'the kingdom of heaven is at hand' (Matthew 3.2).

Once this realization is clear, you don't have to worry yourself interminably about which actions are right. Whether working in a factory or in a kitchen, you can do the will of Christ by giving a cup of water to a thirsty soul. No exceptional deeds are required.

To offer some cool water to a child is a very good Christian action. Why do we ask ourselves complicated questions about what deeds are acceptable?

You cannot keep life alive without letting it live. Let things happen. Don't try to control the universe. Serve the little world around you. A child happens to enter your home. Caress the little one before discussing your business with his parents. You might be a waitress in a restaurant. Serve the customers well. Smile at them. No more right actions are needed.

In whatever you do, keep the great hope. We are not what we are but what we are becoming. We are preparing in menial tasks for a greater calling, to 'serve him day and night in his temple' (Revelation 7.15).

Prepare yourself decidedly for this. In Christ there exists only an 'either/or', never an 'as well as'.

We live in a doomed world. We travel in a sinking ship. Don't analyse the chemical constituents of the water pouring in. Remain quietly on board, fulfilling faithfully your sailor's duty, and prepare for the last swim to the other shore.

Love all those around you, who are so terribly endangered. No one is accepted unless the worst in them is accepted. Love all people just as they are and don't worry about what good deeds to perform. St Augustine wrote, 'Love and do what you like.'

It requires great discipline to be simple. The simplest action is the right one.

22

Having Jesus at His Best

The Evangelists record that Jesus healed a man possessed by demons. They say not one word about how he had come to be possessed by unclean spirits. For them, only his encounter with Jesus is important. He is presented as a man without biography. We know nothing about his past or his family, nor are we informed about what he did after his brief hour with Jesus.

Perhaps in heaven only the minutes we have spent in intimate contact with Jesus will count.

Come to Jesus, and you will discover that you have fulfilled the aim of your life. Come, accepting all he did and does, all he said and says, all he promised, threatened, commanded, and attested by his life.

The manner in which you come will show your intent. Men came to the Garden of Gethsemane with lanterns and torches (John 18.3), which were needed to prevent a false arrest. Today, some approach him with the lights of reason and science, which are indispensable in preventing errors in judgement. But lovers prefer darkness. They come to him without torches, which reveal only the outer man. A lover seeks the real person. Only lovers can know him as he really is.

And what if in the darkness of night they embrace another by mistake? It matters not, because they were destined from the beginning to love not only him but all beings.

The Lord forbade people on several occasions to spread the news that he was the Messiah, because he knew his time had not come. But at a deeper level, he wanted to teach his disciples that men and women can be with him not only when they know they have Jesus with them. They could be with him when in the company of any poor, oppressed, or holy being.

Angelus Silesius wrote, 'Man, if you love something, you love nothing. God is not this and that;

therefore, leave the "something".' St John of the Cross also worried: 'If you stop at something, you are no more committed to the whole.'

Only lovers can explain the enigma: Is Jesus in truth the same yesterday, today, and forever? In the past, he could not bear to see men who might faint because they had nothing to eat, and so he fed them miraculously. Today millions starve. It is not that they faint; they die. Why does he not come to their aid?

Jesus always has the same answer to social problems. The disciples asked him, 'Where can we find bread here in the wilderness for thousands of people?' His reply was, 'How many loaves do *you* have?' (Mark 8.4,5). If the disciples had had more than the minimum required for life, the hunger of others would have been their fault. They had less than the minimum: seven loaves and a few small fish for thirteen men, including Jesus. But they practised self-renunciation, asceticism. Satisfied with their poverty, Jesus performed the miracle of multiplying the food, with much to spare.

Let today's Christians deny themselves and become poor. Then they will see that Jesus has remained the same.

During Jesus' earthly life, there were places where he could not perform mighty works (Mark 6.37). Can it be that through our greed we have created such places in our day?

Come to Jesus, forsaking all. Then you can have him at his best.

23

Influence God

Like every well-organized brain, that of God also has a mechanism for forgetting and remembering. He says, 'Behold, I, even I, will utterly forget you' (Jeremiah 23.39). 'I will also forget thy children' (Hosea 4.6). 'I . . . will not remember thy sins' (Isaiah 43.25).

On the other hand, the groaning of the children of Israel caused him to remember his covenant (Exodus 6.5). The sense of prayer is to bring to God's remembrance things he has known from time immemorial.

Like every unselfish being, the one he forgets most is himself. Therefore our prayers should begin with the words 'Hallowed be thy name'. Usually they start with the request 'Do something for me', which is not right. He needs most to be reminded of himself and of his Kingdom.

There are privileged people who obtain from God everything they desire. It is written, 'The Lord did according to the word of Moses' (Exodus 8.13). More than others, such individuals should say to God, 'Not my will, but Thy will be done.' In the embrace of love we should forget ourselves, as he forgets himself. We need not worry; there will be others to remind him of our existence.

Luther prayed,

> O Lord and good Father, I don't wish to be or not to be, to live or to die, to know or not to know, to have or to lack. Your will be done; I don't wish what is Yours. I wish Yourself. You are not more beloved by me when I have it well, and not less when I have it evil.

God's glory should be our supreme desire in prayer.

The Jews had fled from Egypt in a hurry. They must have left behind many possessions, but not their timbrels. With these they were able to praise God (Exodus 15.20). We may be assured that we can also bring before him our diverse petitions. We can even be very insistent in them. When the children of Israel were in great danger, Moses said soothing words to them, while to God he cried (Exodus 14.13–15). Jesus, too, 'offered up prayers and supplications with strong crying and tears' (Hebrews 5.7).

We are all what we are as a result of influences that impinge upon us. When God requires us to pray, he is essentially asking us to influence him. In this respect he is like us. Let us with determination influence him in favour of the cause to which he calls us.

If prayer moves him, it also influences those for whom we pray. When we kneel in prayer for someone else, we kneel not only before God but also before those for whom we are praying, entreating them thus to follow the right way.

Our prayers influence both God and others.

24

God Who Evolves

Pascal wrote, 'Nature has some perfections to show that she is the image of God and some defects to show she is only an image.'

Mona Lisa could not exist without a model, about whom we know nothing. Leonardo da Vinci's painting proves that real women who sometimes smile wonderfully must exist. Without them we would never have had this admirable image.

Nature is only an image. Therefore an original must exist.

I believe that the ontological argument for the existence of God brought by Anselm of Canterbury (1033–1109) still stands: We have an idea of a perfect being. Existence is an attribute of perfection; therefore a perfect being must exist. This is God.

If everyone's 'I' is incommunicable, how much more is his! Jesus said, 'No one knows the Father except the Son' (Matthew 11.27). When we write about God, therefore, we write about an unknown Being. 'If any man thinks that he knows anything, he knows nothing yet as he ought to know' (1 Corinthians 8.2). We know only a few, a very few, words of God. He is brief, and our knowledge is scanty. Our sermons and books about him must be brief too.

God is known from the Bible under different names. Thomas Aquinas raised the question whether the names predicated about God are synonymous. In his book *Sentences*, he uses for the first time in church history the expression 'attributes of God'. He teaches that the names attributed to God all signify one and the same thing but under many distinctions of reason. We call him by different names only because we apprehend him in manifold ways, but he is one.

This one God has revealed about himself in Scripture not only his almightiness, but also some of his limitations; he is love and cannot love less than to the uttermost. He is immortal. He is invisible. He cannot lie. He cannot get wrathful except with our consent. He said to Moses, 'Let me alone that my wrath may wax hot against the Jewish people' (Exodus 22.24). Because Moses did not let him alone, he did not exterminate the people as he might have otherwise.

There is one attribute of God that makes every quarrel with him appear as senseless as the quarrels with men. God is what he is (Exodus 3.14). He is not what we or he himself would like him to be. He decides all things. He never decided to be the only one to decide all things. He is God. He did not choose to be God, as you did not choose to be a human being, of a certain sex and race, with a certain heredity, born in certain circumstances that will shape your destiny for life. He simply exists.

To him the same words apply that Paul used for himself, 'I am what I am' (1 Corinthians 15.10). God is what he is by nature. Paul was what he was by God's grace. God is the perfect example of a being self-existent, without inner conflict, accepting all his characteristic features, not quarrelling with himself, not desiring the impossible for himself.

For him, too, being means evolving, becoming. The literal translation of the words spoken to Moses 'Ani ehyeh asher ehyeh' is 'I become what I become', not 'what I am'. He knows what he will become. With the qualities he possesses, he could not become less than all in all.

He is basically the same always, but he evolves. A Jewish child of five passing near a church with his father once said, 'Papa, let us enter to see what is new with God.' This is why we should go to church – to receive good news. A pastor who tells only what God was two thousand years ago is not very helpful, since God 'becomes what he becomes'. There is no absolutely changeless object of knowledge and no unchangeable knower, and there is therefore no unchangeable knowledge.

An unknown, an invisible God, a God who evolves –
I cannot comprehend this. When you cannot catch a butterfly with empty hands, you have understood its nature. Knowledge is always only partial and therefore hinders intimacy. 'The Lord said that he would dwell in the thick darkness' (1 Kings 8.12). It is only in darkness that he can be embraced.

If you do not wish a God like this, it would be better to avoid him. Be happy he does not walk with you, because he consumes stiff-necked people in the way (Exodus 33.3).

But if you accept him as he is, then love him with all your heart and with all your soul. This is the first commandment. Everything else comes afterwards.

25

Are You Ready to Die?

Jesus said, 'Whosoever shall confess me before men, him will I confess also before my Father who is in heaven' (Matthew 10.32).

When the Communists took over Cambodia, they entered a church during the Sunday service. Taking the Bible from the pulpit, an officer put it on the threshold. As his men stood by with rifles ready, he ordered the people to leave the building one by one and spit on the Bible. 'Whoever does so will be free to go home,' he said. 'Whoever does not will be shot on the spot.'

Imagine for a moment that you were a member of the congregation. What would you have done under the circumstances?

As one who has passed through similar situations, I know the thoughts that flash through the mind when put to such a test: 'I have a bride. Her heart would break if I were to die. My time has not yet come . . . I have old parents who are invalids. They depend on me for support. They are doomed if I die. Love obliges me to spit . . . So what if I spit? Jesus knows that I have done so under duress. He forgave Peter, who denied him without being in such danger as this. He understands human weakness. In any case, I will spit only a little bit.'

These were people who had come to church to worship God and study his word, but they had never decided to die for Christ. One by one, Christians, who ten minutes before had praised Christ in song, left the church and spat on the Bible. Then came a girl of sixteen. When challenged at gunpoint to spit, she began to weep and said, 'I cannot do it. I love God. The Bible is his letter to us. No child spits on his father's letter.' She knelt down and wiped away the spittle from the cover of the Bible – and fell dead over the holy book, shot in the head.

What would you have done? Many of us have answered a call to come forward to the altar. The altar in Jerusalem was a place where creatures died. Lambs, rams, doves, whatever came upon the altar died. Did you understand your response to the altar call in these terms?

We are not all put in the same situation. Not everyone is forced to lay their life on the line. However, every Christian chose death at his conversion, if it was genuine.

Rabbinical commentaries have said that the key to the Bible lies in the words, 'This is the law, when a man dies . . .' (Numbers 19.14). If a person does not die for the law, they have never really considered it to be the law of God. This is how Christians think, too. A Christian is someone, 'dead to sin' and 'dead with Christ' (Romans 6.2,8). To respond to an altar call means to die to the world. If you have understood this rightly and lived in this spirit, you will make the right choice in times of crisis.

Few of us may be asked to spit on the Bible literally; but to spit or not to spit is a choice we make daily when we are tempted. It means spitting on the Bible, indeed, on Christ, if we wilfully and consciously prefer a sin to his commandments.

Let us choose rather to wipe away the spittle with which others have soiled his holy word and to be faithful at all times.

One Trinitarian God

To Jews and Muslims, the greatest stone of offence in the Christian religion is the belief that the one God is a trinity. Jesus is the first to give a Trinitarian formula to the Godhead. He says, 'Baptize in the name of the Father, and of the Son, and of the Holy Ghost' (Matthew 28.19).

The Church teaches us to worship the unity in the Trinity and the Trinity in the unity. We are not commanded to understand it. In fact, we do many things without understanding them. How many of us comprehend the technicalities of electricity, of cars, of jets, of our household gadgets, of the medicines we use?

Curiously, the early church never said there were three persons in the Godhead. 'Person' is a word used for a whole being. The church fathers who fixed the dogma spoke about three *hypostases* in the Godhead. Etymologically, *hypostasis* means 'inferior' (*hypo*) and 'stand' (*stasis*). Only the three together, Father, Son and Holy Ghost constitute a whole being. There exists no wholeness outside the totality of the Godhead.

Two main accusations are brought against the Trinitarian teaching of the Bible.

1. It contradicts mathematics, which is a discipline that never permits two different series of computation. One plus one plus one can yield only three. Another solution, that one plus one plus one should equal one, is out of the question.

Three persons can surely not be one person, but it does not contradict mathematics to say that three *hypostases*, whatever this word means, or that a divine Father, a divine Son, and a divine Spirit should be one Godhead. Three different entities like body, soul and spirit form one person. Many trees form one forest.

2. It contradicts the biblical teaching that God is one.

Deep biblical truth demands vigorous mental effort and much knowledge. Those who cannot discipline themselves to attain such knowledge are like the fox in Aesop's fable. Unable to breach the fence guarding the vineyard, he said, 'I would never eat such grapes anyway. They are sour.'

Those who have studied know that the Old Testament never speaks about God being absolutely one. The Hebrews have two expressions for the notion 'one' – *echad* and *yachid*. *Yachid* stands for perfect unity. 'I have one only son' would be in Hebrew *yesh li ben yachid*. *Echad* stands for composed unity, as in the expression, '*Vaihi erev vaihi boker yom echad*' (It was evening and it was morning, one day). (Genesis 1.5).

God says that man and wife 'shall be one (*echad*) flesh' (Genesis 2.24). This shows that the word 'one' is not taken in the Bible in the absolute sense.

Elohim, one of the most frequent appellations for God in the Old Testament, is a plural. It could be translated 'Gods', but in Genesis 35.7 and other places, the verb after the subject *Elohim* is in the singular.

After hearing the two distinct dreams of Pharaoh, Joseph says, 'The dream of Pharaoh is one (*echad*)' (Genesis 41.25). He does not even say, 'The two dreams are one.' The two dreams are simply one dream. Many twos can be one. May God grant that we may understand it.

Many Jewish theologians have seen they cannot defend the absolute unity of the Godhead.

The renowned eleventh-century rabbi Gabriol distinguishes between God, his will and his activity in the world, which is something other than his real being, about which we can know nothing. He makes the same distinction that Christian theology makes between *Deus absconditus* (the hidden God) and *Deus revelatus* (God revealed), the same distinction which Hindus made thousands of years before Christ between Brahman Nirguna (God without attributes, that is, without qualities attributed to him by men, which therefore cannot express ultimate reality) and Brahman Saguna (God with attributes).

God can be philosophized about as 'one' in the precise sense of the word only so long as he remains an object of speculation. Those who have a personal experience with God conceive of him as Creator, as Saviour from their sins, and as one who sanctifies them and makes them God-like. The Trinity was experienced in the spiritual life before being fixed as dogma.

Let us adore the whole God, not only one aspect of him. In Hebrew the word for 'face' (*panim*) does not exist in the singular. The Hebrew Bible speaks about the 'faces' of God. We adore not only the majestic face of the serene Father Almighty, but also the face marred by sorrow of the God who suffered for us on Golgotha. We also adore what the Kabbalah calls 'the little face' – the dovelike face that awakens our desire for innocence and goodness.

If we do not understand much, it does not matter. St Augustine, walking along the seashore, reflected on a book about the Trinity that he wanted to write. Hearing a child's cry and fearing something may have happened, he investigated, only to be told, 'I weep because I want to put the ocean in my bucket and can't succeed.' Augustine learned not to expect too much from the reflections of his little mind about the great God.

Through deep thought we can know something of the fringes of the problem. May this suffice and may we be his adorers both in spirit and in truth.

27

A Few Thoughts about the Devil

The Bible calls the devil 'the king of terrors' (Job 18.14) and 'the firstborn of death' (v.13), among many other names. The demons who serve him are usually not given individual names. When asked, one of them said to the Lord, 'My name is Legion' (Mark 5.9).

We know only two possible exceptions. One devil is called Apollyon, the angel of the bottomless pit (Revelation 9.11). The apocryphal book Tobit speaks about a demon whose name was Asmodee. It seems probable that one result of serving the devil is an obliteration of personality.

Demons perform many works on earth. The most insidious is probably that of sowing doubt. It was the devil's first ploy with Eve. Not content with deceiving the race, the devil dared to approach Jesus himself. The Father had said at his baptism, '*This is* my beloved Son' (Matthew 3.17). Every believer receives just such an assurance. After a few weeks, Satan tempted Jesus with the words, '*If thou be* the Son of God' (Matthew 4.3). He uses the same tactic with us.

But he uses even more insidious methods. The Spirit of the Father speaks in a believer (Matthew 10.20), but not always. Satan can also influence a believer to such an extent that he is even able to speak through him. The Lord responded to certain of Peter's words by saying, 'Get thee behind me, Satan' (Matthew 16.23). Jesus discerned that the false thoughts expressed by Peter did not come from his own heart.

Knowing the devil's power, many believers seek some accommodation with him. Montaigne wrote, 'I would burn one candle for God and one for the devil.' This attitude is wrong. My prayer is, 'God, help me every day to be an annoyance to the devil.' We don't have to fear him, in spite of his seeming might. The

Empire State Building is gigantic only when viewed from street level. Christians are seated in heavenly places (Ephesians 2.6). Seen from above, the devils are little creatures.

In Matthew 12.25 and 26 Jesus suggests the best tactic to use in dealing with demons: try to turn one against the other. Split them. The devil of self-satisfaction over one's religiosity can be turned against the devil of whoredom; the devil of thrift against that of gambling; the devil of fear (of being discovered and apprehended) against that of lying and theft.

In times of great demonic oppression and temptation, a simple change of your place of habitation is also effective. Devils are patriots (as were, to an unhealthy extreme, great Satanic personalities like Hitler and Stalin). If you move to another location, they do not always move together with you. A devil besought Jesus not to be sent out of the country (Mark 5.10).

On some occasions, the devil might give you a hard time if you fight him. When forced to leave an individual, he might throw him or her to the ground (Mark 9.20). But devils can be chased away. Subtlety can also be used successfully to outwit them.

Just be aware that the devil (collectively) will plague you until the end of your earthly life. He attacked the innocent couple, the crown of creation, in paradise. He promised them a religious boon: to be like God. He also knew how to keep silent when the threat was too great. He did not contradict God when he was cursed but simply continued his work. He incited Cain and Abel to quarrel about religious matters to make a mockery of religion. He induces men to run after women only because they are beautiful, causing them to forget decency and virtue.

He often uses renowned personalities as tools. Lenin and Hitler both wrote books that shaped the political destinies of the twentieth century. Christianity has not produced many books with such an impact. While Hitler built gas chambers and ovens to kill millions of

Jews, the Church failed to organize a missionary work to bring millions of Jews to conversion.

Hosea well said, 'The revolters are profound to make slaughter' (Hosea 5.2). We are not profound. Therefore many Christians have been led astray, even to the point of helping Hitler and Lenin. Christians sometimes sacrifice to devils while believing they sacrifice to God.

When Jesus said, 'Beware of men' (Matthew 10.17), he meant to be taken seriously. He warns us that there are some people sown in this world by the devil (Matthew 13.24, 25, 37, 38). These are not simply notorious figures like Hitler or Stalin, but ordinary people you might encounter in everyday life.

But don't panic. Remember, the devil will try hardest to make you disbelieve that you are a child of God. My answer to him is, 'Then if I am a child of the devil, I will be an Absalom, a treacherous son to him. I will love God even if I am not his.'

He will also try to make you believe that right is wrong and wrong is right. He will appear as an angel of light to deceive (2 Corinthians 11.14). Again, my reply is, 'Though now I see through a glass darkly, I know whom I have believed and trust him to keep me from falling and to keep all I have committed to him even though my senses deceive me. I will love him even if I cannot see him' (2 Corinthians 13.12; 2 Timothy 1.12).

Scorn the devil. He is a defeated foe, as he knows full well. Jesus conquered him and all his minions on Calvary, for all of us sinners. From the light of Golgotha you can look down on him. I repeat, he is a little creature.

28

Problems of Faith in God

Darwin's most radical claim was that evolution is aimless and without inherent direction. His theory was a biological counterfeit of Adam Smith's *laissez-faire* economics. Smith had argued that a well-regulated, stable and harmonious economy would be the natural result of untrammelled interest actively pursued by all.

We live some two hundred years after the death of Adam Smith. There is no harmonious economic life. Nor could the order in nature result from uncontrolled struggle of all against all.

Why should and how could random evolution produce unselfishness and self-sacrifice — even in the animal world? In many flocks of birds, for example, the first bird that spots a predator utters a warning cry. The flock scatters. The bird has saved its mates by calling attention to itself, sacrificing its life for the good of the flock.

Nature cannot be explained without a Creator. To acknowledge him does not solve all the intellectual problems. There remains the great question mark: If the world was created by a rational Being, why the terrible suffering?

The question 'Why?' addressed to God is as false as the question 'What two even numbers added together yield seventeen?' The book of Lamentations ends with a question: 'Wherefore dost thou forget us for ever, and forsake us so long time?' (5.20). We do not know the reasons for God's doings. We know that he does things that seem strange to us. But he is a God in whom we can trust without understanding him. If we can trust completely in surgeons without understanding what they do, should we not trust in God, the Creator of the surgeon?

I don't claim to understand God, but I know he can do wonders. He made it possible for Jesus to be born miraculously to a virgin. Yet every day he still performs the miracle of making a sperm recognize the ovum. What mechanism prevents the sperm from fusing with any other kind of cell it may encounter? Only the miracle of human conception as orchestrated by God. May this God of miracles do what seems good to him, not what seems efficient or right to me.

While I say this, I also know I have the liberty to pray to God to change his decree. He allows me to pray in the Spirit. The Son prayed in Gethsemane that a decree of the Father be altered. We can do so too.

In either case, we can trust God.

I trust God because he does not boast. He says that he created a heaven and an earth. Now, all earthly rulers praise themselves for the good things they do. But our God tells us about hell too. He could have kept it from us in order that we might love and trust him more. Instead, he tells the truth as it is. We can trust him.

He freed the Jews from the Egyptian bondage, proving he could deliver his people. He did not free the Jews from the Nazi holocaust. It was not that he lacked the power. He must have good reasons to proceed differently in each circumstance. In any case, he takes full responsibility for everything that happens.

All kinds of theological arguments can be given to explain the existence of so much evil in the world of a good God. These valuable explanations are like a finger pointing to the moon. But to see the moon you have to look beyond the finger. Then you become silent. Questions are no longer relevant. You realize that there are answers that only time will reveal and that the purposes of God will one day become obvious.

The unrighteous opium war waged by the British against China opened up the country to the inrush of missionaries. Access to inland China for evangelization was the result of the Arrow War in 1856. God nullified good counsel and allowed wrong decisions to be made (2 Samuel 17.14) in order that David, his anointed, might return to his kingdom. Thus we learn not to accept all God's guidance. He gives the wicked guidance that will destroy them. Rather, we should do what the Bible teaches about how to be pleasing in his sight.

I admit that it is not easy to walk with this God. Sometimes he says very unpleasant things. He tells Adam that certain things are forbidden, Abraham that his descendants will be slaves in Egypt for four hundred years.

You will wonder about his words. Aristotle said, 'Wonder is the starting point of philosophy.' It is the starting point of religion too. From wonder we advance to an acknowledgement of our utter dependence upon God. We – humankind – cannot escape his will.

Nor should we try to escape his will. What we focus on determines our character. The more exalted the object about which we think, the more Godlike we become. It is good for humankind to think primarily about God.

Every concept is an image of an object. When the Father forms a notion, he thinks perfectly about his own divine nature. Thus his idea, the Word, expresses his nature completely. We know him as the Son. The two love each other perfectly. The Holy Spirit is this love. St Bernard of Clairvaux called the Holy Spirit the kiss between the Father and the Son.

Let us therefore bow before the Holy Trinity. Then let us add to their love our own. In love we will find the answer to our restless questionings.

29

In the Name of Jesus

Whatever is said about Jesus in the Bible concerns every believer because Jesus identifies himself organically with believers. 'Christ is the head of the body' (Colossians 1.18), and we are the members (1 Corinthians 12.12).

The Romans had a saying, *'Actiones et passiones sunt suppositorum.'* (Actions and passions belong to the person.) It is not the hand that steals but the thief; not the hand that gives alms but the philanthropist; not the heart that loves or hates but the whole person. Likewise, every action and passion of Jesus is also mine, and vice versa.

Divine charity is not his alone; I possess it too, because the spirit that animates him belongs to me. There is no problem, no burden of mine that is not also his. My sins do not belong only to me; they are automatically his too and crucify him afresh (Hebrews 6.6).

We have everything in common. We are both twice born, but in reverse order. He was born first as the Son of God and then became man: I was born first as a human being and then as a child of God. This is the difference. Otherwise we are one body.

Human life has been given to me as a boat to cross the sea from nonexistence to heaven. This is the spiritual sense of the many episodes in the Gospels of the disciples' travelling by ship across the sea of Galilee. Jesus is the good navigator, who also stills contrary winds. To resist being totally and consciously a member of his body is like committing suicide.

We often begin or end personal prayers and public services with the words 'In the name of Jesus', which means with a readiness for sacrifice after his example, or rather, together with him.

When we pray 'Hallowed be thy name' to God, we are saying in effect, 'Give me the grace of self-sacrifice that others, seeing its beauty and knowing that it arises out of love for you, might be drawn to adore you.' The sacrifice is meant to be complete. Jesus said, 'Greater love has no man than this, that a man lay down his life for his friends' (John 15.13). This is the ultimate sacrifice for a man. Jesus went further: he died for sinners, for his enemies. Since God's children belong to a different order of being, their love has the same ultimacy as that of Jesus: self-sacrifice in the service of their foes.

Jesus would not elaborate on this teaching. He had taught people to love their enemies. They asked him how a man could be released from the heavy duty of loving his own wife. How far love must go belongs to the many things Jesus left unsaid because his disciples were not yet able to bear them.

He is so far beyond us that it is only natural for communication to be difficult. Doubts arise too in many things connected with him. There is nothing wrong in doubting. The wrong lies in sharing the doubts with anyone other than Jesus himself. Speak with him about them as the followers of John the Baptist did: 'Art thou he that should come, or do we look for another?' (Matthew 11.3).

He will teach you how to love to the uttermost and reveal to you the mystery of his doings. If you love like Jesus and become one with him, people will be offended by your deeds as they were offended by his commanding a Jew to carry a load on the Sabbath. In the case of that man, a natural law had been broken. He had been healed in a moment after thirty-eight years of paralysis and was able to carry a mat on his shoulders. The natural laws come from the same God who ordered us to keep the Sabbath. If the first were broken, why not the latter?

With Jesus, we are in a sphere that humans cannot judge; the realm of the supernatural. Christ's ministry engendered in Herod the reaction that he was John the Baptist come back from the dead, in the Pharisees that he was in a pact with the devil, in his relatives that he was beside himself (Mark 3.21), in Peter that he was 'the Son of God'. The qualities that called forth so many reactions must have been beyond the ordinary. We believe the only explanation is that he was – and is – God incarnate.

Spinoza wrote, 'That God would assume human nature, I must confess seems to me as absurd as that a circle assumed the shape of a square.' To which I would respond with the words of Tertullian: 'I believe it because it is absurd.' A child can take a piece of string and shape it like a circle, then reshape it like a square. We have to accept on faith the fact that God can do things that surpass the imagination or reason of the greatest genius.

The most intimate disciples of Christ do not understand everything yet. St Ignatius, bishop of Antioch, before his martyrdom said, 'I am burdened with chains, but I am only a beginner in the Church of Christ.'

Faith tells us that Jesus is God. He is love to the uttermost, and he calls us to such love, even towards our enemies. He is one head and we are his body. We are one.

30

Reason and Sentiment

Only one half of the human brain directs logical thinking. It is the left hemisphere where the treasury of words is located. The right hemisphere is the seat of pictures and dreams. Strangely, it is this half that more quickly provides a solution to the serious problems of life.

Reason is not reliable. The Romanian word for 'mind' is 'liar'. A fox that once lost its tail in a trap tried to persuade the other animals that it was much better not to have a tail. We also tend to propose as objective truth ideas that would serve to justify our past biographies.

A multitude of depraved sentiments exert a detrimental influence on our reasoning. We all agree that two and two are four, that it is warm when the sun shines, and that the USA has a president – but only because these truths don't interfere with our own interests and passions.

Hobbes said, 'Even the axioms of geometry would be disputed if men's passions were concerned in them.' Lenin also wrote, 'Men would contradict that two and two are four if it conflicted with their interests.'

Truth can be very unpleasant when memory tells me, 'You have sinned', and pride says, 'It is not so'. Pride almost always succeeds in convincing memory. Reason is at hand to offer powerful alibis. Francis Bacon said it in *Novum Organum*: 'The human understanding is no dry light, but receives an infusion from the will and affections, where proceed sciences which may be called "sciences as one would".'

People even become martyrs of a religion they embraced only because it happened to be the religion of their sweetheart. One of the top leaders of a terrorist gang in West Germany killed and went to prison because the boy she loved was a revolutionist. This was

83

her only motive for embracing the most radical ideas.

Christ refuses faith in him engendered by such motives. He counsels those who plan to build a tower to sit down first and count the cost, and advises kings who intend to make war to consult first whether they are able to win (Luke 14.28–31). He endorses the wisdom of people who, in building a house, dig deep and lay the foundation on rock (Luke 6.48). In effect, he is saying they must make sure they have the right motives and serve the highest causes.

He urges us to follow him only if we have full proof that faith in him is right. He exempts those who don't have the evidence from the duty to hold this faith. 'If I had not done among them the works which none other man did, they had not had sin,' Jesus said (John 15.24). You are without excuse only if a clear revelation has been given you.

However, let us always remember that one part of our mind can apprehend the truth quickly without relying on the processes of reason. It is the same part that induces Romeo to consider Juliet the only girl worth living and dying for and makes Don Quixote forsake all for Dulcinea. God must be loved with all the heart. Therefore, this part of the mind has to convince the other half of its validity, while admitting the possibility of distortion due to emotional complexes of sympathy and antipathy, which block truth.

Reason can adduce proof that adultery is love, that theft is wise provision, that unbelief is intellectual honesty. 'Every way of a man is right in his own eyes, but God weighs the heart' (Proverbs 21.2). Because we don't have a strong grip on truth, with hearts committed to the desire for truth alone, many churches are able to resort to the ways of the world with considerable success.

Before apprehending truth, your reason must become truthful. Without cleansing the mind of passion, you render the grasp of religious truth virtually impossible.

84

31

Why Evil in the World of a Good Father?

Anyone who reads the Bible is invariably struck by the sheer volume of evil and suffering it recounts, in particular the suffering of the innocent. To many people this poses a grave problem.

The simplest answer to the question 'Why is there so much evil in a world created by a good God?' is, 'We do not know.'

Hayyim ibn Mussa (1390–1460), a Spanish rabbi, tells how he heard a renowned preacher attempting to explain why God acted as he did and speculating about his deeds. 'Thereupon', the rabbi said, 'misfortune came upon me in a great pogrom in Seville. I was beaten and wounded until my persecutors desisted because they thought I was dead. And here you are speculating about God and his decrees. I have greater faith in the sufferings which God imposes upon us than in your theories about them.'

Is it not enough to endure pain and persecution and natural catastrophes? Must we endure philosophical explanations too?

Job, upon receiving news that he had lost all his property and that all his children had died, exclaimed, 'The Lord gave, and the Lord has taken away; blessed be the name of the Lord' (Job 1.21). When God gives, he gives in mercy; when he takes, he takes in mercy. About mercies we need to jubilate and not to speculate.

An evil can often be a blessing in disguise. Edison, thought to have an addled brain, was driven out of school. A train conductor who beat him made him deaf. This affliction closed him to external influences. He could draw from inner wells. As a result, we owe to him the electric light bulb. More than that, he earned a patent every fortnight.

Lincoln was grieved because of two bankruptcies. Through these God showed him that he was made for something better than commerce. He became one of the great presidents of America.

There have been many artists of unsound mind. Over seventy analytical papers have been written about the folly of Van Gogh alone. Yet would his art have been possible without this touch of madness? Neither the Romanian poet Eminescu nor the Hungarian Ady Endre could have created their masterpieces without the incipient folly in them.

Some artists have been aware of their weakness and loved their perilous handicaps. Edward Munch said, 'I want to keep my weaknesses. They are a part of myself. I wouldn't want to miss suffering. I have to give much thanks to this suffering in my art.'

I once saw a performance of an old classical Japanese dance. Its subject was a young king of such beauty that wherever he appeared all activity stopped. No one could do anything but hold their breath while gazing at the king's splendour. His appearance negated the possibility of a normal existence for anyone else. His subjects could no longer love one another because they compared their neighbours unfavourably with the beautiful king. For the good of his citizens, then, the young king had to wear an ugly mask.

Do you understand the significance of this story? Could human relations and falling in love and the world itself exist if we were able to see our God in all his majesty? He too had to wear an ugly mask by taking the form of sin-sick humanity. In the person of Jesus, God appeared among us with 'no form nor comeliness'. He had 'no beauty that we should desire him . . . We esteemed him not' (Isaiah 53.2,3). Thus he made it possible for us to esteem one another's beauty and desire after the love of our fellows.

Think about this story. It might help you somewhat to make peace with the existence of evil in a world created by a good God.

32

God's Characteristics

Men dress God in the garments of their age. He was described as a despot when the world was ruled by despots. He has been successively portrayed as a slaveholder and an English country-gentleman. Scientists conceived of him as a great geometrist, a great mechanic. Today some say he is a great revolutionist. In a male-dominated society, he surely must be male. Modern-day feminists call him 'she'.

These extrapolations are very much out of touch with God as described in the Bible. The last impression one retains after a lifetime of study is that God is an unfathomable mystery.

We have the assertion 'God is love' (1 John 4.8), but it must be a love entirely apart, because he takes the responsibility for actions not normally performed by a loving being. God says, 'I will corrupt your seed' – think only of the tragedy of having bad children – 'and spread dung upon your faces' (Malachi 2.3). For the sins of certain priests, whether a few or many, he puts the whole priesthood under a curse in the same chapter.

When village children hear the song 'There's a wideness in God's mercy like the wideness of the sea,' they think only of the breadth of the millpond. But navigators accustomed to travelling the seven seas would understand better. Astronauts would doubtless think in terms of the limitless ocean of space. But there is something wider than the universe, and that is the spiritual realm, in which God is not limited to our human concept of goodness.

We see God neither as he is nor as he would like to be. One of our impressions is that the God who created our universe is a sad God. Lucifer had just rebelled, drawing with him a third part of the 'stars' of heaven (Revelation 12.4). The fall of man followed. We deal with a sad God who repents of having created our species and is grieved (Genesis 6.6). Our God is also wearied. 'Ye have wearied the Lord with your words' (Malachi 2.17). Jesus, 'the express image of God' (Hebrews 1.3), was also 'a man of sorrows, and acquainted with grief' (Isaiah 53.3), and knew weariness while on earth. John's Gospel records that once he sat on a well in Samaria, 'being wearied with his journey' (John 4.6). He had left Jerusalem upon hearing news about dissension over his and John's baptism and was now among strangers. Bone-tired, hungry and thirsty, he was indeed a man of sorrows. If we don't realize this, his words will sometimes appear strange and incomprehensible.

But look! A woman comes to draw water, alone, in the heat of the day. She is despondent and weary of life. She has had six husbands, including one stolen from another's marriage. None of them could give her joy. But immediately the weary Son of God forgets his own sadness and becomes a comforter to her (John 4.4–42).

Let us not create images of God according to the *mores* of our society or our own status. Meeting the tired God, the one crucified every day afresh by his followers (Hebrews 6.6), let us forget our own deep sorrows and be a comfort to him.

May I add that the present meditation needs to be taken with a grain of salt. I too am a weary man who has known much sadness, and I show God as I see him. I paint him with sombre hues, knowing that 'now we see through a glass, darkly, but then' – praise God! – 'face to face' (1 Corinthians 13.12). And I know that one day a happy God 'will wipe away all tears from their eyes; and there shall be no more . . . sorrow, nor crying' (Revelation 21.4).

88